❧ READING THE PAST

LEONARD COTTRELL

READING THE PAST

THE STORY OF DECIPHERING ANCIENT LANGUAGES

CROWELL-COLLIER PRESS, NEW YORK

Copyright © 1971 Leonard Cottrell
Copyright © 1971 The Macmillan Company

All rights reserved. No part of this book may be
reproduced or transmitted in any form or by any means,
electronic or mechanical, including photocopying, recording
or by any information storage and retrieval system, without
permission in writing from the Publisher.

Library of Congress Catalog Card Number: 73-153762

The Macmillan Company
866 Third Avenue
New York, New York 10022
Collier-Macmillan Canada Ltd., Toronto, Ontario

Printed in the United States of America
10   9   8   7   6   5   4   3   2   1

TO DOCTOR JOHN CHADWICK, M.A.
IN FRIENDSHIP AND GRATITUDE

❧ CONTENTS

Contents

❧ READING THE PAST

❧ INTRODUCTION

Have you ever wondered how the human race first got the idea of writing? We take reading and writing for granted. At school we learn our ABC, and soon become familiar with the letters of the alphabet; probably we remember that the word *alphabet* comes from the first two letters of the ancient Greek writing system, *alpha, beta* (our *A* and *B* signs). But apart from that we accept the idea of writing and reading as naturally as the act of breathing, or eating. There seems nothing remarkable about it.

Now we know that Man has existed for at least a million years, during which time he learned to speak, to communicate ideas and thoughts, whereas his fellow animals never got beyond the stage of making noises. Yet it is only during the past five thousand years, at most, that in a few favored places Man learned the art of putting onto some material signs and symbols which when read by another man who understood the system would convey the sounds of spoken language, and enable people living hundreds of miles apart to communicate with each other.

In other words, if you think of the million years of Man's existence as represented by one month, the invention of writing dates from the last three hours of the last day of that month. Until then, the only knowledge Man could inherit from his ancestors was that passed on by word of mouth by the wise old men of the tribe and memorized by their successors. And then just a few men in certain places found out how to represent, by written symbols incised on clay, painted on potsherds, carved in stone, or perhaps written in ink on papyrus (the ancestor of paper, from which the very name *paper* is derived) facts and ideas which, instead of dying or being passed on by word of mouth, would never perish as long as the writing survived. The knowledge and wisdom of generation after generation could be passed on, so that even in our own time, not thirty years until 2000 A.D., we can read the thoughts of men who lived on this earth in 3000 B.C.

Of course there was a long process of development behind this invention. These ancient scribes, in Egypt, Mesopotamia, and Crete, obviously did not write in English, German, French, Hungarian, or any language which is in use today; they were not invented. The scribes of those lands in those far-off times spoke languages which have, for the most part, long passed out of use.

How, then, did modern scholars learn to decipher and read these languages, and so put themselves (and us) in touch with people who died perhaps four or five thousand years ago? This is the subject of this book. We shall try to explain how the art of writing came into existence; how and why it developed among certain peoples whom we call "civilized" while remaining at a primitive level elsewhere; how it was possible for scholars of the nineteenth and twentieth centuries A.D. to decipher these ancient languages; and something of what we have learned, as a result of these researches, about the lives, customs, and beliefs of the ancient Egyptians, the Sumerians and Babylonians, the Hittites, and the inhabitants of Minoan Crete and Mycenaean Greece.

You may well ask why we should confine ourselves to a small island in the eastern Mediterranean, to the narrow strip of the Nile Valley, to the valleys of the Tigris and Euphrates. What about the rest of Europe? What about India and the Far East? What about North and South America? The answer is that we shall, in passing, mention the development of writing, or the beginnings of non-oral communication, in these countries or continents, but we have to recognize that the art of writing in its most sophisticated forms began in the areas we have mentioned. Moreover, in these areas the first civilized communities developed, and since they were interesting civilizations, besides being the oldest on earth, what the ancient writings tell us about them is of profound interest and importance.

In short, the purpose of this book is not primarily to explain the invention, growth, and development of the art of writing throughout the world, but first to focus our attention on those areas of the earth's surface in which Man first developed the craft of representing spoken words in terms of written symbols; second, to show how those symbols were first deciphered in modern times; and third, to indicate what those symbols reveal to us of the way of life of people who died forty or fifty centuries ago.

LEONARD COTTRELL

3

1 ✍ MAN'S MOST BRILLIANT INVENTION

Perhaps the title is an exaggeration, but if not *the* greatest, writing is certainly *among* the greatest inventions of mankind, even though we take it for granted. We think of the computer and the rocket as among Man's most brilliant inventions, though they are rapidly becoming commonplace. However, the invention of writing has probably given a greater impetus to Man's progress than any idea which has entered his head during his million years of existence.

It is now generally accepted that our remote ancestors were akin to the ape family, although it is not true to say that they were apes. But at some time roughly computed as a million years ago, they came down from the trees and learned to walk upright. In evolution there is something called *specialization,* which means that the body concentrates on developing one particular part. Our ancestors "specialized" in the enlargement of the brain. The human foot did not develop very much, whereas the hands improved greatly, because Man, now walking upright, developed his hands so that they could fashion tools and weapons. But his brain developed to an even more remarkable degree, and its cubic capacity increased. Man also developed his vocal organs far beyond those of the lesser animals, so that instead of merely making noises he could, in time, develop speech, which enabled him to communicate with his fellow men.

We know that the lesser animals also communicate. They have mating calls; they can produce other sounds which mean danger or fear. But the whole apparatus of vocal communication found, for instance, among birds and cattle and dogs, is rudimentary. With Man it is different. He learned to use his vocal organs in a much cleverer way, so that in time he could exchange not merely emotions such as grief and fear and pain, but a whole range of ideas. A cat or dog can, through its voice, communicate fear, alarm, love, and pain: the dog's bark of joy at greeting his master, or anger when a stranger approaches, the cat's plaintive "mew" when it wants food or is in distress and its contented purr when it is happy. But neither of these animals, nor any other animal save Man, can do what I am doing on this sheet of paper—put forward ideas which have nothing to do with grief, pain, fear, or love.

The process by which Man learned to express himself in speech must have been a long one, and we can only guess how it happened. "The gift of tongues," as it used to be called, was at one period considered so important as to be miraculous: e.g., the famous Bible story of how the Lord's disciples were suddenly endowed with this gift by God's

5

command. People once regarded speech, along with many other things, as a direct gift from God. If one takes the religious viewpoint it was indeed God-given, in that all things come from God; but the process by which it was acquired, over scores of thousands of years, was a slow one. The art of writing came only at the end of the long period during which speech was developed. The ancient Egyptians thought that writing came either from Isis, sister of Osiris, one of their greatest deities, or from the ibis-headed god Thoth who was also the god of wisdom. To the Babylonians, the god of writing was Nebo, son of Marduk, the greatest god. In Greece the deity who endowed men with the gift of writing was the messenger-god Hermes.

One fact is certain, that the art of passing on information and ideas by word of mouth developed with the increasing capacity of Man's brain. In many ways Man is inferior to the so-called lesser animals. For instance, his nasal organs are rudimentary, because though other animals continued to rely very much on their sense of smell, to Man it was less important. Physically he is a weak creature compared with, say, the lion, the tiger, and even the gorilla to which he is remotely related. He has not the speed of the jaguar; he cannot fly unaided; in water his movements are clumsy compared with those of a fish. The strength of his limbs is puny compared with that of a lion's. Yet he has developed a brain which enables him to subdue all these creatures, and it was through his superior mental equipment that he developed the gifts of speech and eventually writing. He is, as a famous philosopher said, a "tool-making animal," and in the words of Dr. Galliani, who lived in the time of Louis XIV (1638–1715), he is "the only animal which takes an interest in things which don't concern him."

6

However, countless thousands of years ago, when our primitive ancestors began to speak, they probably began by imitating the sounds of other animals. Even today, when we use the word "cuckoo" or "whip-poor-will" we are imitating the sounds made by those birds, and when children talk of a "bow-wow" they are crudely imitating the barking of a dog. This is the idea underlying what is called the onomatopeic theory, after the Greek word *onomatopeia*, the basis of which is that human speech began by the imitation of sounds. But there is another belief, firmly held by some linguists, that primitive Man made sounds like "pooh-pooh" to express a feeling or emotion, and that these sounds came in time to express that feeling to all men and women. This is known, frivolously, as the "pooh-pooh" theory, and no one can be certain which of these two theories is correct. Perhaps both are.

For the origins of speech one must depend on theories rather than known facts. In comparatively recent times objects have been given the names of the men who made or used them, and perhaps this happened in ancient times. The sandwich was named after an English aristocrat, the Earl of Sandwich. The woollen garment called the "cardigan" takes its name from another aristocrat, the Earl of Cardigan, just as wellington boots take their name from the Duke of Wellington. As P. E. Cleator aptly comments in his book *Lost Languages,* "We are content to munch what we call sandwiches, but steadfastly decline to make a meal of cardigans or wellingtons."

However, it is most probable that the earliest words were related to animal sounds and gestures. It is also very likely that speech did not begin to develop quickly until men began to live in permanent settlements, where they

7

saw more of each other than when they were wandering hunters, and where they needed to communicate ideas to each other somehow.

This would explain why the art of writing, which is only a way of making speech permanent and capable of being transmitted far beyond the range of the human voice, appears to have begun in Egypt and Mesopotamia. I say "appears" because, to date, it is only in these two areas that we can trace the invention of writing back to before 3000 B.C. The apparent reason for this is that in these favored regions men first learned to live together in permanent settlements.

Of course this does not mean that in Egypt and Mesopotamia Man suddenly had the idea of writing with pictures, or that picture writing of a primitive kind does not appear in other parts of the world. But these earlier attempts were not writing such as we know it and the Egyptians and Sumerians (of lower Mesopotamia) knew it—a unified system governed by a set of rules which have to be learned. For example, signs have been found scratched on cave walls which obviously represent things: sometimes the heavenly bodies, sun, moon, and stars; sometimes, in fact very often, animals on which Man depended for his food before he learned to cultivate plants. Or in a trading agreement maybe a man agreed with another that in three months' time he would exchange with him an ox for four sheep. If he scratched or drew on a piece of stone or clay pictures of three moons (for three months), an ox, and four sheep, that would be sufficient for the man with whom he was doing business to recognize the agreement. But only that other man would understand the pictures; this was not yet a universal language.

Because of his wonderfully developed hands, Man

learned scores of thousands of years ago to carve in bone and no doubt in wood, to draw and paint on cave walls (like the famous ones at Lascaux in France), to make the drawing and carving tools, and to mix the necessary paints. None of the lower animals have ever done this, though the most advanced modern apes, given a paintbrush and a surface to work on, can sometimes produce crude compositions which might be called designs.

The main point is that long, long before the first true examples of writing appeared along the valleys of the Nile, the Tigris, and the Euphrates, men had learned to express themselves in speech. There were thousands of languages, all different, though some tended to fall into groups having common characteristics. But although Man had begun to draw pictures of such things as the sun, moon, stars, animals, plants, and his fellow men and women, no one had yet conveyed through signs the actual sounds of a language, so that other men, seeing these signs, would sound the language in their heads and be able to understand whatever message the signs were intended to convey. We call this a phonetic script after the Greek word meaning "sound."

Then true writing began, significantly, in two regions of the Middle East. There large communities of men and women had learned to live together, building towns and villages and settling down instead of wandering perpetually in search of wild game, as their ancestors had been forced to do, and as most of their contemporaries in other areas were still doing.

2 ⸲ EGYPT – KNOWN AND UNKNOWN

It may seem strange that Egypt, the home of one of the two oldest known civilizations on earth, should have kept the secret of its writing system until the early part of the nineteenth century, not more than one hundred and fifty years ago. After all, Egypt is frequently mentioned in the Old Testament, parts of which, like the story of Moses and the Children of Israel, go back to well before 1200 B.C. Presumably Joseph spoke the ancient Egyptian language, since Biblical tradition states that he was employed by the pharaoh in high office. Whether he could also write is another matter. It may have been the strict preserve of the priests and priestly scribes.

The Greeks began to settle in Egypt as far back as the seventh century B.C. The country was well known to Homer, author of the two great Greek epics, the *Iliad* and the *Odyssey*, which are set in a period at least twelve hundred years before the birth of Christ.

The Greek historian Herodotus, who paid long visits to Egypt in the fifth century B.C., tells us much about the life and customs of the ancient Egyptians of that period, but it is obvious that he could not read the language. In a passage from his *Histories* describing the Great Pyramid he says:

> There is an inscription in Egyptian characters on the pyramid which records the quantity of radishes, onions, and garlic consumed by the laborers who constructed it; and I perfectly remember that the interpreter who read the writing to me said that the money expended in this way was 1,600 talents of silver.

This shows that Herodotus, though an educated Greek, could not read ancient Egyptian, and that neither could the "interpreter," since from what we know of the type of inscriptions which the ancient Egyptians placed on their still-surviving monuments, they certainly would not have wasted time and space on such trivialities as the amount of vegetables consumed by the workmen. The so-called interpreter who talked to Herodotus nearly twenty-five hundred years ago must have been the ancestor of one of the modern "dragomans" who hang around the pyramids with tall tales to beguile tourists! Whatever inscriptions may have existed on the ancient limestone casing-stones which once covered the Great Pyramid have long since disappeared, since these stones were removed by Arab looters to help build Cairo.

Even in Herodotus' time, about 450 B.C., comparatively few people, such as the priestly scribes, could read ancient

Hieroglyphics were splendidly engraved on this wall from the Temple of Karnak in Central Egypt.

Egyptian writing. When the Romans came in the first century B.C. Egypt had already been ruled for more than three centuries by the Ptolemaic kings, who were Macedonians and spoke Greek. These Macedonian rulers, of whom Cleopatra was the last, probably spoke the Egyptian language as well; however, they most likely did not write it, but conducted their correspondence in their own Greek language, which is much easier to learn and write. The Romans wrote and spoke in Latin, and during the four centuries of their occupation the ancient Egyptian language, which had been spoken and written for more than three thousand years, finally died out.

So for something approaching fourteen hundred years this curious anomaly existed. The written and spoken languages of Greece and Rome survived, and indeed survive down to the present day; Greek and Latin inscriptions could still be understood; Greek and Latin literature continued to be read by educated people. Yet throughout the eight-hundred-mile length of Egypt there were stupendous monuments, many of them elaborately carved with inscriptions; within the tombs were found scrolls of papyrus filled with writing. Yet although Egyptian civilization had flourished five times as long as that of Greece or Rome, it remained mute for fourteen centuries. It could only speak to posterity through its magnificent pyramids, temples, tombs, and other monuments.

The decline of the ancient writing system, until in the end it could no longer be read, was due in part to the Koptic Christians. When the Roman Empire, of which Egypt formed a part, became officially Christian in the fourth century A.D., Egypt also was Christianized, and the Egyptian Christians known as Kopts (or Copts) became sufficiently powerful to close all the ancient temples and disband the scribal schools where writing was taught. Then in the seventh century A.D. the country was conquered by the armies of Mohammed, and it has remained a Moslem land down to the present day, apart from a small Koptic minority. The Moslems were indifferent to any past save their own, and often deliberately defaced ancient Egyptian statuary because their religion forbade the representation of any human being.

The Kopts were no better. Besides closing the temples or converting them into Christian churches (as one can see for example in the Luxor temple and the temple of Ptah at Karnak), they sometimes hacked out the faces in Egyptian tomb paintings, which they regarded as heathen idols, and turned the tombs into homes. As for the strange signs and symbols with which these tombs and monuments were inscribed, the Kopts were completely indifferent to them.

However, in one extraordinary way the Kopts did do something to preserve the ancient writing, though quite accidentally. When the Moslems conquered Egypt they successfully imposed their own religion, language, and culture on the majority of the population. Most Egyptians learned to speak Arabic and worship Allah in the mosques which were rapidly built throughout the land. But although the Kopts had to learn Arabic to converse with their fellow countrymen who had adopted the language, they retained elements of their ancient language in their Christian church rituals, and also in some words and phrases in common use. In fact, the Arabic spoken by the ordinary Egyptian peasant today, whether Moslem or Kopt, is somewhat dissimilar to the Arabic of (for example) Syria, because it has absorbed a number of words and phrases which we now know are of

15

ancient Egyptian origin. *Kopt* is one of them. This important fact has to be borne in mind when later we consider how Champollion and other early nineteenth-century scholars succeeded in deciphering the ancient Egyptian writing system which the Greeks called *hieroglyphs*.

3 ✆ THOMAS YOUNG, THE PIONEER

The ancient Egyptian writing system is usually called *hiero-glyphic*, and the symbols *hieroglyphs*, a Greek word meaning "sacred signs." We now know that there is nothing particularly sacred about them; they are as practical in their purpose as our own ABC. But this false idea that the ancient Egyptian hieroglyphic writing was in some way "holy," an idea which began in late Greek times and continued through the Middle Ages and the Renaissance, misled Egyptologists for centuries. It is curious that this idea should have arisen, since the ancient Egyptians themselves were probably the most materialistic race that ever lived. There is nothing mysterious about their language, religion,

17

or customs, apart from the basic fact that their language remained undeciphered for fourteen centuries.

Probably the fact that in the Greco-Roman period (ca. 500 B.C.–300 A.D.) the hieroglyphs were generally used for religious inscriptions led to this erroneous belief. Both Herodotus and Diodorus described the hieroglyphs as "sacred letters," as distinct from the "popular letters" of what was known as the demotic script. In fact there were three forms of Egyptian writing, called in Greek the *hieroglyphic*, the *hieratic*, and the *demotic*. All these scripts represented the same language, but whereas the first, the hieroglyphic, was "picture writing," used mainly for carved inscriptions on monuments, the hieratic was an abbreviated form of the same script, comparable to modern handwriting and adapted for writing on papyrus, and the so-called demotic script was an even more abbreviated form, developed in Greek times and roughly comparable to modern shorthand. But basically all represented the same language, and there was nothing more sacred about the hieroglyphs than there was about the hieratic or demotic forms.

But when the scholars of the Middle Ages and the Renaissance began to pore over copies of these ancient Egyptian texts, seeking for a clue to their decipherment, they were strongly influenced at first by the writings of Greek and Roman scholars who lived when the ancient Egyptian writing system was in rapid decline or had perished altogether. One such author, the Greek historian Plutarch (46–120 A.D.), in his book *On Isis and Osiris*, says that the pictorial or hieroglyphic form of Egyptian writing was used for sacred writings, comparable to the maxims of Pythagoras. On the other hand, the Jewish historian Josephus (37–95? A.D.) said that among the inscriptions to be seen on Egyptian monuments were historical accounts of wars, battles, and sieges, they were therefore not entirely religious.

There was also a certain scholar named Horapollo, the reputed author of a book called *Hierogliphika,* the only surviving translation of which has been dated to the fifteenth century A.D. He purports to give a translation into Greek of all the familiar hieroglyphic signs found on the monuments. He says, for example, that the figure of a goose stands for "son" because that animal is greatly concerned with its offspring, and that the figure of a hare means "open" because a hare's eyes rarely close. Both these interpretations we now know to be nonsense, yet they made sense to our medieval ancestors, and why not? However, Horapollo was right about the translations of some signs. Why, then, was he sometimes right and sometimes wrong? Probably because he was mixing knowledge with imagination, as many writers are prone to do. He may have gained some of his accurate knowledge from the manufacturers of charms and amulets engraved with the ancient writings, to whom the knowledge had passed by tradition, and made up the rest for himself.

Throughout the sixteenth, seventeenth, and eighteenth centuries A.D. the problem of the Egyptian hieroglyphs continued to exercise the minds of certain scholars, but usually without fruitful results. One exception was Athansius Kircher (1601–1680), a professor of mathematics who after careful analysis of the Koptic language became convinced that it preserved, in alphabetic form, the language of the ancient Egyptians. He was not far wrong. Unhappily, Kircher persisted in believing that the monumental inscriptions were of a sacred nature, so that when he tried to use Koptic writing to unravel the mystery of the hieroglyphs he was led hopelessly astray. When he came to study inscriptions on the Pamphilian obelisk, he translated the seven signs of the Greek title *Autocrator* as:

> The author of fruitfulness and of all vegetation is Osiris, whose productive force was produced in his kingdom through the holy Mophta,

which is pure rubbish. *Autocrator* was simply the Greek royal title comparable to *King*, and nothing more. Nevertheless most of Kircher's fellow scholars accepted his judgment, if only because their ignorance was even greater than his.

In the eighteenth century one or two scholars began to suspect that certain signs were phonetic: that is, they represented the sound of a spoken word and did not necessarily denote the object depicted by the sign. As an example of this, imagine, in modern times, being confronted with a picture of a man and a date (from a date palm). If you were an ancient scribe who was accustomed to picture writing and also knew English, you would not think of the figure of a man as meaning a human being but only the sound of the word *man*. Similarly, a picture of a date would not mean the fruit but merely the sound *date*. Putting the two sounds together you would get the word *mandate*, which has nothing to do with either men or dates. This is what is meant by the phonetic system on which most modern languages are based, though we have long ceased to use pictures to convey our meaning.

A similar and more obvious example is the word *belief*. We spell it in alphabetical letters, but if we employed a phonetic script based on pictures, we would require only a picture of a bee and a picture of a leaf, both readily recognizable, as seen on the following page. To the skilled scribe the meaning of these two symbols, dependent on their position in relation to other symbols, would not be "bee" and "leaf," but the idea of belief, trust, faith. This is the principle of phonetic writing at the stage when the symbols have ceased to be pictograms and become phonograms.

One important clue was picked up by certain eighteenth-century savants. Egyptian hieroglyphic inscriptions often contain a number of symbols enclosed within a flattened oval, like this:

In fact it represents a double coil of rope with a vertical extension at one end; later it was rendered as an oval. It was suggested, as a guess, that whenever this sign—which French scholars called a *cartouche*—occurred it enclosed the name of a king, queen, or other royal personage.

In 1798 the Emperor Napoleon invaded Egypt with a large army, and took with him among his entourage a number of distinguished French scholars with a special interest in ancient Egypt. In the following year, 1799, French soldiers stationed at Rosetta, one of the two main branches of the Nile where it flows into the Mediterranean, discovered a block of basalt inscribed in hieroglyphics, demotic, and Greek. In all three parts of the inscription the cartouche appeared, and scholars who studied the inscribed stone suspected that in the Greek part the flattened oval did contain the name of a king, the Macedonian pharaoh Ptolemy V Epiphanes; the date was 196 B.C.

In a short while the British defeated Napoleon's troops

at the Battle of the Nile. Soon afterwards the Rosetta Stone, as it came to be called, was "liberated" by the British soldiers, and is now one of the most precious possessions of the British Museum. But before that happened, copies had been made and distributed to French scholars and others throughout Europe. They rapidly realized that this was a *bilingual* inscription; it represented the same statement rendered in Greek, the language of the court circles at the time, and in two forms of the ancient Egyptian language, the hieroglyphic and the demotic.

The importance of this piece of stone is obvious, although the inscriptions on it were damaged and incomplete; because if, as it appeared, each of the three inscriptions conveyed the same meaning, then it should be possible to find out the phonetic values of some of the Egyptian characters. For instance, since the name *PTOLEMY* or *PTOLEMAIOS* occurred in the Greek inscription inside a cartouche, then where a cartouche appeared in the hieroglyphic or demotic part of the inscription it should be possible to decide which of the Egyptian characters represented the sounds *P, T, L, M,* and *S.* Following the same method, it would, in theory, also be possible to establish the value of other Egyptian characters.

The Greek inscription, which could of course be read easily, emphasized the good things which Ptolemy V Epiphanes had done for Egypt. Some scholars were misled into thinking that the Egyptian demotic script was alphabetic, whereas we now know that it was not. A copy of the three inscriptions was sent to a noted French Orientalist named Sylvestre de Sacy, but he made little progress with it. However, he showed it to another Orientalist, a Swedish diplomat named Akerblad, who had better results. He identified most of the names in the demotic version by comparing them with their equivalents in the Greek version. He correctly rendered such words as "temples," "Greeks," "he," "him," and "his."

Even greater progress was made by an English physicist named Thomas Young (1773–1829), the discoverer of the wave theory of light. Young was full of enthusiasm, a skillful mathematician and an accomplished linguist. He and the Frenchman Jean-François Champollion must be regarded as the first true decipherers of the ancient Egyptian writing system. Young, it is said, had learned to read by the time he was two, and before he was twenty had mastered twelve foreign languages. But linguistics was not his only interest. He published papers on the habits of spiders, the atmosphere of the moon, a theory of tides, and diseases of the chest. But once he had received a copy of the Rosetta Stone, he became obsessed with the decipherment of the hieroglyphic system.

He started by cutting up his copy of the inscription into pieces and then pasting the thirty-two lines of the demotic text onto separate sheets of paper. He knew that Egyptian writing is read from right to left, and made allowance for this when he assigned each group of Egyptian signs to those Greek words to which he suspected they corresponded. Like his predecessors de Sacy and Akerblad, he was helped by the fact that certain words were repeated several times in the Greek version, for instance *Ptolemy, Alexander,* and *Alexandria.*

4 ∾ THE GREAT CHAMPOLLION

Up to this point no scholar had made a serious attempt to tackle the hieroglyphic portion of the Rosetta Stone because they tended to accept the ancient belief that these were mysterious sacred symbols. They concentrated on the decipherment of the demotic form of the script in which Young had made great progress. Also, the demotic version was much fuller and less damaged. Nevertheless quite a few people began to wonder, since the demotic script was evidently a translation of the Greek version, whether the hieroglyphic inscription also carried an identical message, and if the three scripts could be correlated.

In the year 1790, eight years before Napoleon's invasion of Egypt, there was born at Figeac, in the Departement du Lot, France, an extraordinary child. He was christened Jean-François Champollion. He was the son of Jacques Champollion, the librarian at Figeac, and his wife, whose pregnancy was attended with such illness that her desperate husband called in a local sorcerer named Jacuou. Jacuou laid Champollion's young wife on a bed of burning herbs of which he alone claimed to know the properties, and told her, "From your travail will be born a boy who will be light of the centuries to come."

When the child was born, the doctor who delivered the baby was astonished to see that its face had an olive tint, that the eyes were black and the hair dark, like an Oriental's. Even the whites of the eyes had the yellow tinge characteristic of Levantines.

Jean-François grew up in an era of revolutionary struggle. In the third year of the republic his father became a superintendant of the municipal police at Figeac. At a time when France was in tumult, Jacques Champollion's house often became a refuge for those whose lives were in danger, and one of these, the Benedictine Dom Calmet, later became the youngster's teacher.

The atmosphere in which the child developed was one of anxiety and sometimes terror. On one occasion when a particularly fierce storm was raging the two-and-a-half-year-old Jean-François could not be found. After a frenzied search of the house his parents eventually discovered him "high in the attic against dormer windows like a house-martin between two beams, head outstretched and arms widespread. In this position, like some young Prometheus, he seemed to be trying to catch 'a little of the heavenly fire' as he explained to his terrified mother."

As the son of a librarian he grew up surrounded by books, and their effect upon his agile, sensitive mind was enormous. His elder brother, Jacques-Joseph, who was also highly talented, taught Jean-François and became, as one writer has truly said, "the first mediator between Jean-François Champollion and his Promised Land, Egypt." Then in 1798, the year Napoleon invaded Egypt, the elder brother was transferred to Grenoble. This beautiful city had a splendid university and excellent schools and was truly the intellectual capital of the region. Three years later Jean-François, then aged eleven, joined his brother in Grenoble and began to study Hebrew. A year later he astounded his tutors by interpreting a passage from the Bible in the language in which it was written. And in the same year there arrived at Grenoble the great Jean-Baptiste Fourier, one of the leading scholars working in Egypt under Napoleon.

Through Fourier the child Champollion was given access to the famous memorial of the Napoleonic Commission, the *Description de l'Egypte*. Fourier, struck by the knowledge and enthusiasm of the boy Jean-François, showed him his collection of Egyptian antiquities. The effect was almost miraculous. From that moment Champollion determined to penetrate the mystery of the hieroglyphs and applied all of his powerful though immature intellect to the task. "Enthusiasm alone," he wrote later, "is the real life."

He learned the Koptic language from Dom Raphael, a former Koptic monk whom he met at Fourier's house. And it was through Fourier that he was enabled, at an early age, to leave the constricting atmosphere of the semi-military *lycée* (school) which he attended, and begin studies far in advance of those normally considered suitable for boys of his age. Fourier lent him rare and valuable books, and when he was fourteen years old Jean-François had begun to write his first scientific paper, "Egypt under the Pharaohs." On September 1, 1807, he read his introduction to the learned gentlemen of the Grenoble Academy. At the end of his address the President embraced the boy and said in a congratulatory speech:

> We like to think that you will justify our hopes, and that one day your works will make a name for you and that you will recall your first encouragement from this Academy.

When Champollion was sixteen he moved to Paris to continue his studies and also to seek a suitable job, because in the meantime he had fallen passionately in love with the sister of his brother's wife. She was six years older than he was, and he wrote of her at this time:

> Each to his taste and leanings
> But I think in this life
> The wisest man of all
> Is the man who takes a wife.

He had, as will be observed, a sentimental streak in his nature, as have many scholars.

It was at this period that Champollion met the austere Orientalist Sylvestre de Sacy. De Sacy, then forty-nine, was at the peak of his career. There were also many distinguished Orientals in Paris and Jean-François, because of his swarthy appearance, was often mistaken for one of them. There was the Koptic priest Jeach Scheftidshy, a member of the Koptic Union who recited Mass in Koptic at the church of Saint-Roche. Jean-François often listened to him, familiarizing himself with the Koptic tongue. He wrote at this time:

> I want to know Egyptian as well as I know French. I am in fact a Kopt who for his amusement translates into that language everything that comes into his head.

27

In 1808 Champollion was given the opportunity of seeing a copy of the inscription on the Rosetta Stone, which greatly stimulated his imagination. He did not at first attempt to decipher the hieroglyphs, which he like his predecessors continued to regard as "sacred signs." But quite early on he recognized that there was an intermediate script between the demotic and the hieroglyphs which he called "hieratic." He had studied a number of ancient Egyptian papyri written in this form of writing. At first he thought that the hieroglyphics came first, then the demotic and then hieratic, but soon he acknowledged his mistake. He came to realize that hieratic was the first cursive form of the hieroglyphic script, adapted for writing on papyrus, and that demotic came later, as a development and shortening of the hieratic.

When he was only eighteen years old, his Egyptological studies were interrupted by his appointment to the Chair of History at the newly created Faculty at Grenoble. Although many of the students were his former schoolfellows and even his former schoolmasters, his eloquence and knowledge quickly captivated them. Despite his new academic duties at Grenoble, he continued to find time to study the ancient Egyptian writing system. It was then that his familiarity with the Koptic language came to his assistance. In the year 1813 he made a discovery of profound importance, though to us it may seem simple. Think of what we call personal pronouns—words like *him, his, her, hers.* Champollion was now completely familiar with the endings of the six personal pronouns in the Koptic language. In his opinion these should also have occurred in ancient Egyptian. When he came to examine the hieroglyphic portion of the Rosetta Stone he found, corresponding to the Greek word for "he," the symbol for the horned serpent. In the de-

The Rosetta Stone inscribed in hieroglyphics, demotic and Greek gave linguists the key to Egyptian hieroglyphics.

motic text he found a sign which was derived from the horned serpent and was identical with the Koptic *f* of the third person.

It may not seem to be of great importance, but Champollion, in determining only one hieroglyph according to its phonetic value, had taken a big step forward towards the final decipherment. Nevertheless, he did not immediately follow this up. In fact, he took several steps backward by continuing to believe that most of the hieroglyphic signs were "sacred signs" with no essential phonetic value. He believed at this time, for instance, that the hieroglyphic sign showing a lion, in the middle of the cartouche surrounding the name *Ptolemaios,* stood for the word "war" which in Greek is *p(t)olemos,* whereas we now know that it stands for the sound *l* and nothing more.

During the years following 1813 the young scholar became embroiled, as do modern students, in urgent political affairs. He was a great admirer of Napoleon and became suspect as a Bonapartist at the time when the emperor returned from Elba for the Hundred Days. Champollion was suspected of treason by the Grenoble authorities and for a time wandered, a hunted and homeless man, in the Alpes Dauphinés. He lost his post at the university, as did his brother, but in the end, after overcoming many dangers and difficulties, he was appointed a schoolmaster in Grenoble and was able to resume his studies. In 1821 he embarked on what may seem to us a simple experiment. He counted all the signs in the hieroglyphic part of the Rosetta inscription and compared the count with the symbols in the Greek part. He discovered that there were three times as many signs in the hieroglyphic section as in the Greek one. This was sufficient to prove that it was impossible for each hieroglyph to represent a whole word. The hieroglyphic text, like the demotic, was almost certainly phonetic.

As we have seen, the young scholar already knew the phonetic values of many of the demotic signs, which he had obtained through the Greek part of the inscription. He had also studied samples of the hieratic form of writing from other sources, because by this time examples had been found written on papyrus scrolls found in the tombs. Now he began, as a further experiment, transliterating the demotic signs first into the hieratic form and then into hieroglyphs. The critical word was *Ptolemaios*. He suddenly realized, because of his familiarity with the Koptic language, that the Egyptian form of this was not *Ptolemaios*, as Young had believed, but *p-t-o-l-m-j-s*, the sound of which was *Ptolmis*.

Here was the evidence for which he and other scholars had been waiting. Champollion's transliteration of the name *Ptolemy* or *Ptolemaios* (to give it its Greek form) was as follows:

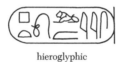

hieroglyphic

demotic

□ p   △ t   ⅾ o   ↞ l   ⊏ m   ⏛⏛ i   ⌐ s

The uppermost part of the diagram shows the demotic and the hieroglyphic forms of the name, and the lower part shows each Egyptian hieroglyphic symbol followed by its equivalent in our own Latin alphabet.

This was all very well, but if only he could find another well-known name containing some of the same symbols! That would have been irrefutable proof. Fortunately Champollion was familiar with the demotic equivalent of the name *Cleopatra*, which contains the consonants *k-l-p-t-r*, in that order. It will be noticed that the sounds *p, t,* and *l* also occur in the name *Ptolmis*. If Champollion could find a hieroglyphic inscription with a name in a cartouche which he could identify as that of Cleopatra, then he would find the same symbols but in a different order.

In Egypt at about this time, 1814, an English collector of antiquities named William John Bankes had found an obelisk and its base at Philae, south of Assuan, with a bilingual inscription in Greek and hieroglyphic. The Greek part of the inscription bore the name *Cleopatra* within the usual cartouche. In 1815 Bankes made a copy of the hieroglyphs, and the obelisk and base were transported to England and made available to Young, who apparently could do nothing with them. But when in 1821 Champollion was at last enabled to see a copy of the Philae inscription, he realized that he had found the clue for which he had been waiting. He recognized the name *Cleopatra* and its hieroglyphic equivalent. In fact, not only was Cleopatra's name to be seen on the Philae monument, but also that of Ptolemy. And when he compared the symbols within the two cartouches, sure enough they were in the positions where he had hoped they would be. It was, as his biographer Barleben writes, an electrifying moment.

On the following page is the cartouche of Cleopatra followed by the phonetic equivalents of the symbols according to Champollion's decipherment.

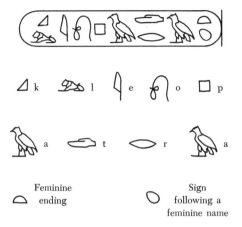

From these two cartouches Champollion now had no less than twelve Egyptian signs which could be accurately identified with Greek letters, the phonetic values of which were known. His many years of arduous study, hindered at times by political troubles and later by ill health, were bearing fruit at last. He went on, using this method, to identify the hieroglyphs in some eighty royal cartouches, including those of such well-known rulers of the Greco-Roman period as Alexander the Great, Domitian, Tiberius, and Trajan. Yet it had to be admitted that these were Greek or Roman names rendered into ancient Egyptian. Could it be that the hieroglyphs were only used, at this period, for the rendering of such foreign names?

The answer came on September 14, 1822, when the scholar received impressions of some bas-reliefs discovered in an Egyptian temple which undoubtedly pre-dated the period of Greek occupation, though by how long was then not known. Several cartouches appeared in the inscription, among which was one on the next page.

33

Champollion was familiar with these signs from his research, and knew their phonetic values. He also knew that the first sign, representing the sun, stood for the sound *Re* in Koptic. His fingers trembled as he held the paper and pondered over the other two signs. According to his calculations the sign rather like a modern *M* stood for the sound *m*, and the two crook-like signs for the sounds *s-s*. Could this possibly be the cartouche of the great pharaoh R-M-S-S—Rameses? Then he came to another sign in which the two latter signs were similar to those in the first, like this:

But Champollion knew that the first sign in this cartouche, representing the ibis, stood for the god of wisdom, Thoth. Therefore, read by his method, the name would be *Thothmes*, that of a great Egyptian king (in fact several bore the name), which was rendered into Greek as *Tuthmosis*. He now understood that the hieroglyphic signs, once considered so mysterious, were a combination of both phonetic signs and those symbolizing objects.

A short while after this discovery he read to the French Academy his historic *Lettre à M. Dacier relative à l'alphabet des hiéroglyphes phonétiques* but did not mention his latest discovery, reserving it for his great publication *Précis du système hiéroglyphique* in 1824. In this he said the mode of writing employed by the ancient Egyptians was a complex system which was "figurative, symbolical and phonetic in the same text, in the same phrase, in the same word."

For eight more years Champollion worked on his epochal discovery which, after a lapse of more than fourteen centuries, would enable the ancient Egyptians to speak directly to the modern world. He spent two years in Egypt, copying inscriptions; he visited Turin and other cities where Egyptian collections were kept; he never halted in his labors, despite failing health, until suddenly in 1824 he had a heart attack from which he died, at the age of forty-one. His devoted brother Jean-Jacques took over the task of completing and publishing his books, *Grammaire égyptienne* and *Dictionnaire égyptien*.

Since those years generations of Egyptologists have worked on the hieroglyphs, and are still working to this day, because the ancient language, though now largely comprehensible, still presents many problems. Not the least of these is the fact that the Egyptians rarely used vowel sounds; in the main they used only consonants. The ancient scribe, knowing the context in which the word appeared, would recognize its pronunciation and meaning. We cannot always do this. To take a simple example in English, think of the words *many* and *money*. If in either case the word was simply spelled *m-n-y*, how would we know what it meant? Only by studying the place in which the word appeared in the sentence, and then only if we were lucky. That is why there are still disputed readings of ancient Egyptian texts, and if any reader decides to take up the study of ancient Egyptian writing he will still have some formidable problems to solve.

After Champollion's death other notable contributions

were made to this branch of Egyptological research, especially by the Italian scholar Rosselini, the Germans Richard Lepsius, Ludwig Stern, and Adolf Erman, and by the British scholars K. Sethe, Sir H. Thomson, H. Grapow, and the late Sir Alan Gardiner. All have acknowledged their debt to that baby born in 1790 with his sallow complexion, dark curly hair, and black Oriental eyes, whose mother was told by the sorcerer Jacuou, "From your travail will be born a boy who will be a light of the centuries to come."

5 ⁊ THE
BIRTH OF
EGYPTIAN
WRITING

Young, Champollion, and the later decipherers tackled the
interpretation of ancient Egyptian writing from the bilingual Greco-Roman inscriptions (ca. 350 B.C.–300 A.D.) in
which the hieroglyphs appeared alongside an almost identical Greek text. But once scholars understood the fundamen-
tals of the ancient writing system they could read far older
Egyptian inscriptions going back as far as 3000 B.C. A whole
world which had been invisible for fourteen hundred years
could become known. It was no longer a question of pondering over the monuments with their indecipherable inscriptions. The ancient Egyptians could speak directly to us,
and since they had written a great deal on their temples

and tombs, and on papyri buried in the tombs, much information became available.

However, Sir Alan Gardiner has written that "Egyptian history is a collection of rags and tatters." One might also compare it to a long winding river in which islets appear at scattered intervals. Some of the islets are big, and some small. Some are widely separated, others lie close to each other. Our knowledge of Egyptian history from both the monuments and the documents is like the islets in the river; there are very large gaps in between where our knowledge is scanty or non-existent. Also it must be realized that this new information from inscriptions only supplemented that obtained by archaeologists, whose skill lies in interpreting evidence from objects alone, although usually they have at least a working knowledge of the language.

There has always been, and probably always will be, a friendly rivalry between the linguists, who interpret ancient writing systems, and the archaeologists, who are concerned mainly with objects—not only temples and tombs, but pottery, artifacts of stone, copper, bronze, and iron, statuary, tomb furnishings, and so on. When, as often happens in Egypt, these objects are also inscribed with the ancient writings, the information derived from them is all the greater.

After a period of about one hundred fifty years since the ancient Egyptian writing system was first deciphered, we can look back on the enormous panorama of Egyptian history, extending over three thousand years, and see it in perspective. Nevertheless there remain many gaps to fill, and dating, particularly of the early pre-Dynastic and Archaic periods, must remain vague and partly conjectural. This is because Egyptian chronology is based on the reign-lengths of the pharaohs, records of which were kept by the priests. These records, of which there are several, are incomplete and differ in some details.

There is also a record made by Manetho, a Greek-speaking Egyptian who lived in the third century B.C. during the reign of Ptolemy II. He was a priest of Heliopolis and had access to records long since destroyed. Manetho wrote a history of Egypt which has been lost except for a few extracts quoted by later historians who lived six hundred years after his death, but these extracts include a list of Egyptian kings from the First Dynasty (ca. 3200 B.C.) down to his own time. He divided his pharaohs into thirty-six dynasties, giving each the name of the region from which its ruling family originated. This was a considerable achievement.

As for what happened before the first pharaoh of the First Dynasty (ca. 3200 B.C.), we have to depend largely on what the research of archeologists can tell us. It seems that from about 5000 B.C. on, or perhaps even earlier, groups of people who had previously been wandering in search of wild game came upon the Nile Valley and settled in considerable numbers. For them the valley had two main attractions: the abundance of game which lived along the river, and the annual flooding of the Nile which brought and deposited on its banks its gift of fertile mud. These tribesmen, who had already learned the arts of agriculture and husbandry, were accustomed to growing their crops and pasturing their flocks and herds at desert oases, and then wandering on, much as the Bedouin Arabs do today.

But when they came to the Nile Valley they found wild game which lived in or near the Nile, perpetual fertility (except during the season of flooding) so that two crops a year could be grown, and an abundance of fodder for their animals. The early settlers, who were at the Neolithic (New

Stone Age) stage of development, bred cattle, sheep, and donkeys, and grew barley and emmer (a coarse form of wheat) and stored it in mat-lined pits which have been found by archaeologists. Their hunting weapons were bows with flint-tipped arrows, spears, likewise flint-tipped, stone axes, and maces. They reaped their crops with wooden sickles set with flint "teeth" and used stone hoes for digging. These implements have been found by archaeologists who have excavated their settlements and given them names like "Amrataean" and "Badarian," according to the names of the sites at which these tools were first found.

These facts, on the surface, may seem to have little to do with the invention of writing; but in my opinion they have, because the earliest use to which writing was put was almost certainly the keeping of records. It began in a very mundane fashion, as we shall see further when we come to look at the civilization of ancient Crete. In ancient Egypt, from an early date, the various tribes scattered along the great river learned to cooperate with each other in the building of canals and embankments to control the flooding, and quite possibly in measuring the annual rising of the river. By measuring and keeping records of the inundation the inhabitants could foretell whether this year there would be a "good Nile" or a "bad Nile," whether the flood level would be too high or too low. A very high Nile would mean disastrous flooding; too low a Nile might mean famine.

From the reign of the first pharaoh records were kept, and remains of these Nilometers, though of a much later date than Hor-Aha, exist in Egypt today. But some form of measuring device probably existed even earlier, in what we call pre-Dynastic times. It was necessary to keep records not only of the rise and fall of the Nile but of numbers of cattle, quantities of grain and other food, and annual crop yields, and to identify stuff stored in pots with an appropriate sign or signs. Earthenware pots dating from before the First Dynasty have been discovered painted with such signs; archaeologists have also found pictures of ships, animals, men, and gods painted on cliffs and cave walls.

During the period before Egypt was unified, the various tribes along the river sometimes fought with one another, and at other times became allies. The time came when the entire land was roughly divided into two kingdoms, that of northern or Lower Egypt, stretching from the Mediterranean southward to a point a little to the south of modern Cairo, and southern or Upper Egypt, extending from the Egyptian delta as far as Assuan. Writing began to develop shortly before the accession of the first pharaoh to rule the whole of Egypt, Hor-Aha. His reign began in about 3200 B.C., though again this is a conjecture with which not all Egyptologists agree.

Shortly before the accession of Hor-Aha, or Menes, as he was named in much later Greek inscriptions, there began to appear alongside or within these pictures of objects little signs which are clearly distinguishable from the surrounding pictorial representations. As Sir Alan Gardiner wrote in *Egypt of the Pharaohs:*

> The images are the same in both cases, mirroring all kinds of material objects such as weapons, plants, animals, human beings, and even the gods themselves. The emergence of hieroglyphs, as the miniature signs are called, was due to the fact that there was much which people wished to communicate which could not be exhibited visually, such as numbers, proper names, and mental phenomena. This supplementary character persisted, side by side with others, throughout the whole of Egyptian his-

tory, so that when, as often happened, the scenes in sculptural reliefs were furnished with explanatory hieroglyphic legends, the latter might be fairly said to illustrate the former rather than vice versa.

It is difficult to render ancient Egyptian writing in terms of modern English; however, imagine that the English language did not exist, but that you wanted to write down the sentence "I love Rose." You could express it with these symbols:

Each of these three symbols is a picture of an object, but you do not want to say "eye, heart, rose." The reader would look at these symbols not as pictograms but as phonograms and ideograms. *Eye* is a phonogram and stands for the first person "I," the heart would be an ideogram meaning "love," and the rose is another phonogram standing for the name of your beloved.

Before and during the reign of Hor-Aha and his successors of the First Dynasty one can almost see the hieroglyphs developing before one's eyes, so rapid was the process. But the difficulty in reading the hieroglyphs, unlike, say, Latin or Greek which use alphabets, is due to the fact that the Egyptian signs sometimes stood for the object represented, sometimes for the sound of a word, syllable, or consonant, and sometimes for an idea.

By about 2700 B.C., when the Great Pyramid was built, ancient Egyptian writing had already assumed the form which it was to retain for some three thousand years. It was also written on papyrus, the earliest known form of paper, which required a modification of the hieroglyphic symbols to make them adaptable to the flowing or hieratic writing when a scribe used ink and a reed pen instead of laboriously carving on stone. Such papyri, made from the papyrus plant which then grew abundantly beside the Nile, have been found in tombs, and most of them were of a religious nature.

But there were other writings, works of fiction, proverbs, and poems, which give us a much better idea of what the ancient Egyptians thought and believed than their somewhat monotonous and repetitive tomb and temple inscriptions. Fortunately a few of these documents have survived and have been translated.

6 ~ WHAT THE ANCIENT EGYPTIAN WRITINGS TELL US

About six hundred miles upriver from the Mediterranean stands the small town of Assuan, at a point where the Nile, hurrying north from the Sudan, breaks in white foam over smooth granite boulders and sluices through channels in the rock, forming swift-flowing rapids. It is a dramatic landscape, worthy of what was for thousands of years the southern frontier of Egypt. Here ruled the Lords of the Elephant-nome (*nome* meaning a province of Egypt) who were responsible for guarding the frontier against incursions by the southern tribes, and often for mounting expeditions into the south in search of ivory, gold, and giraffes, monkeys, and other rare animals to furnish the royal zoos.

We know this from inscriptions discovered in certain

rock-cut tombs of these nobles near Assuan. There is one made for a certain Harkhuf, who describes himself in the inscription as a caravan conductor. He lived in the reign of the pharaoh Pepi II which began around 2250 B.C., though this date, like those of most of the early pharaohs, is largely conjectural. "Caravan conductor" is, of course, only an approximate translation of the word inscribed in the tomb, and means that Harkhuf led troops of soldiers with pack animals into the regions of the south at the behest of his royal master the pharaoh.

Pepi II lived for ninety-nine years, according to the records, but at the time recorded in this inscription he would have been a boy of perhaps ten or eleven. He had evidently set his heart on acquiring a "dancing dwarf" known as a *Deng*, almost certainly a member of the pigmy tribe which still inhabits part of Central Africa. This does not mean that Harkhuf and his companions ever penetrated so far south, but that they bought the *Deng* from some tribe they met in the southern Sudan. To them the unfortunate pigmy was an object of trade. The boy pharaoh was so delighted to hear what Harkhuf had brought back to Egypt that he wrote him a long letter, of which the caravan conductor was so proud that he had it inscribed on the walls of his tomb. Here is part of the inscription in Sir Alan Gardiner's translation:

> Thou hast said in this thy letter that thou hast brought a Deng of the god's dances from the land of the Horizon-dwellers like to the Deng brought by the god's seal-bearer Bawarded from Pwene in the time of Izozi; and thou has said to My Majesty that never had the like of him been brought back by any other who has visited Yam previously. Truly I know that thou passest day and night taking thought for me. . . . My Majesty will perform thy many excellent requests so as to benefit the son of thy son

eternally, and so that all people shall say when they hear what My Majesty did for thee; "Is there the like of those things which were done for the Sole Companion Harkhuf, when he returned from Yam, on account of the vigilance which he showed to all that his Lord loves and praises and commands?" Come north to the Residence at once. Hurry and bring with thee this Deng. . . . If he goes down with thee into the ship, get stalwart men who shall be around him on the deck, beware lest he fall into the water. Also get stalwart men to pass the night around him in his tent, and make inspection ten times in the night. My Majesty desires to see this Deng more than all the tribute of the Mine-land and of Pwene.

The latter part of the inscription is one of those very few instances when an authentic human voice can be heard penetrating the clouds of official verbiage in which the message is presented. Most Egyptian tomb inscriptions, including that of Harkhuf, consist of boastful rhetoric. They are anxious to tell us how important the owner of the tomb was, what high offices he held under the pharaoh, and how highly His Majesty esteemed his excellent qualities. But occasionally something breaks through in this case the impatience of a young boy who has been promised a fine present and cannot wait to see it. One feels that it was Pepi, and not the scribe, who wrote the letter.

Here is another touching example from a tomb inscription which dates from the reign of Amenophis II (ca. 1436–1413 B.C.), nearly a thousand years after Pepi II. The tomb is that of Amenemhab, an old soldier who had fought in many campaigns under Amenophis' father, the great warrior king Tuthmosis III, as well as under the reigning pharaoh. Amenemhab was one of the oarsmen in the royal barge during a festival at Thebes, which was then the capital of

Egypt. Evidently the Pharaoh suddenly recognized the old soldier, who proudly records:

> His Majesty noticed me rowing wonderfully with him in his vessel, "Khammat" was its name. I was rowing with both hands at his beautiful feast of Luxor, likewise to the splendors of (part missing). . . . I was brought to the midst of the palace; one caused that I should stand before the king Amenophis II. . . . I bowed down immediately before His Majesty; he said to me "I know thy character; I was abiding in the nest while thou wert in the following of my father. I commission thee with office that thou shalt be deputy of the army as I have said; watch thou the élite troops of the King!

One might ask, "Were these two trivial incidents worth all the trouble of deciphering ancient Egyptian?" Of course not. They are quoted only as examples of the occasional gleams of humanity which shine through official chronicles. The main value of the decipherment has been to establish the overall pattern of Egyptian history, so far as it can be established; to identify monuments according to the kings or nobles who built them, and whose names appear on them; to read the wall inscriptions and the papyrus scrolls hidden in tombs which tell us a great deal about Egyptian religion and funerary customs; to examine and translate the rare works of literature which have survived, and which tell us more than the monuments can about how the ancient Egyptians thought about life and death, about love and marriage, children, and many of the problems of living which still affect us today.

What kind of society is revealed by the documents, inscriptions, and physical monuments, and how does it compare with those of Greece and Rome? First, it was in the utmost degree hierarchical. There was never at any time in its history anything approaching a popular assembly, nothing resembling the Greek democracies or the Roman senate. Ultimate power resided in the person of the pharaoh who was regarded as the "son of Re" (the sun-god) and therefore semi-divine. His only rivals were the powerful priests, but as the king was also the chief priest he usually managed to retain ultimate control of the kingdom. Attached to the temples were the scribal schools; only through attending them could a man become literate, and literacy was the key to power.

You could, without being literate, be a common soldier, or a farmer, a baker, a smith, or some other kind of tradesman. But if you aspired to anything higher then you had to learn to write, and that was not easy. Fortunately there have been preserved certain school exercise books in some of which the scribe admonishes his pupils who neglect their studies. Here is part of one, in which the scribe compares his lot with that of the farmer:

> I am told you have abandoned writing and taken to sport, that you have set your face towards work in the fields and turned your back upon letters. Remember you not the condition of the cultivator faced with registering the harvest-tax, when the snake has carried off half the corn and the hippopotamus has devoured the rest? The mice abound in the fields. The locusts descend. The cattle devour. The sparrows bring disaster upon the cultivator. The remainder that is on the threshing-floor is at an end, it falls to the thieves. . . . And now the scribe lands on the river-bank and is about to register the harvest-tax. The janitors carry staves and the Nubians rods of palm, and they say "Hand over the corn" though there is none. The cultivator is beaten all over, he is bound and thrown into the well, soused and dipped head downwards. His wife has been

bound in his presence, his children are in fetters. His neighbors abandon them and are fled. . . . But the scribe is ahead of everyone. He who works in writing is not taxed, he has no dues to pay. Mark it well.

This well-known passage illustrates several interesting facts about ancient Egypt. First, its wealth came mainly from the land, and taxation was not in currency, which had not yet been invented, but in kind. Secondly, the word *scribe,* which we encounter so frequently in Egyptian literature, does not mean merely a man who writes. It means an official, who could be a tax collector like the one in the above passage, or a "Scribe of the Army," in charge of stores and equipment, like a modern quartermaster, or he could be a priest. They were all scribes, and the one thing they had in common was their ability to read and write, a qualification so rare and valuable that, with a few exceptions, such as army officers, it was the only way to attain high office in the state.

The passage about the unhappy cultivator also illustrates only too clearly how bureaucratic ancient Egypt was. It was run by officials in an elaborate hierarchy of rank extending from the nobles surrounding the pharaoh to the lowest grade of tax collector. And this system persisted throughout the three thousand years of Egypt's history, with little change, right down to the time of the Ptolemies and the Romans. The ordinary people had no say in the governing of their country or the choice of their rulers.

Another characteristic of Egyptian civilization was its conservatism. In the entire history of mankind there has been no civilization so tradition-bound, so resistant to any kind of change, except perhaps that of China until recent times. For three thousand years, as we know from the tomb paintings, the carved monuments, and the writings which

*A relief in chalk of Egyptian scribes
dates from around 1350 B.C.*

50

enable us to date these monuments, Egyptians spoke the same language, worshipped the same gods, and wore the same kind of dress, though slightly modified among the aristocracy after the Eighteenth Dynasty. The mass of the population lived in the same kind of mud brick dwellings, cultivated their land with the same kind of tools, accepted unquestioningly the same beliefs and customs, from the time of Menes in 3200 B.C. down to the coming of the Romans in the first century B.C.

To take a simple example, most of us have seen in museums little statuettes in the form of Egyptian mummies, usually made of faience (glazed baked clay) or sometimes of wood. These are known as *ushabtis* (answerers) and were buried in tombs, sometimes in large numbers. Their function was to act as servants of the dead, since by a process of sympathetic magic they became living human beings in the afterlife. Inscribed on them is a spell. The dead man is speaking:

> O *Ushabti*, if I am called upon, if I am appointed to do any work which is done in the necropolis (cemetery) . . . even as a man is bound, namely to cultivate the fields, to flood the river banks or to carry the sand of the East to the West, then speak thou "Here am I!"

The people in whose tombs such statuettes were placed, and these included kings, had probably never done a day's manual labor in their lives. These *ushabtis*, with the identical spell inscribed on them, are found in tombs dating from 2500 B.C. down to 200 B.C., always in the sepulchres of men and women of rank. Why? Because there had been a far-off time, long before the first pharaoh came to the throne, when there were no kings or nobles, and practically every able-bodied person had to take a hand in digging irrigation canals and carrying "the sand from the East to the West." That was probably in about 5000 B.C.; but such was the fear of the noblemen that they would have to do menial tasks in the afterlife that they continued to have these statuettes, who were substitute laborers, buried with them right down to Ptolemaic times.

There is another significant example of Egyptian conservatism in the so-called Pyramid Texts found inscribed on the walls of the burial chambers of certain pharaohs of the Fifth Dynasty. Here lay kings buried with the utmost pomp and ceremony in stone-lined burial chambers within stone pyramids of enormous size. Yet among the texts is the exhortation to the king to "throw sand from thy face!" when he is born again in the afterlife. Authorities have suggested that this is a distant memory of the time several thousand years before the pyramids were built, when even chieftains were buried in simple pit-graves in the desert sand, such as have been found in great numbers on pre-Dynastic sites.

None of these facts could have been known but for the decipherment of the writing system. The decipherment has also enabled us to understand Egyptian burial and funerary customs, and something of the fundamental religious beliefs upon which these were based. Greek and Roman writers have told us much about the care which the ancient Egyptians lavished on the preservation of their dead bodies, and mummies have been dug out of tombs for centuries to furnish European and American museums. But it was only when the ancient writings were deciphered, those inscribed both on tomb walls and on papyri hidden in the tombs, that the real significance of these customs was recognized.

Throughout their long history the Egyptians worshipped literally thousands of gods. Besides the principal deities, Re, god of the sun (or in later times Amun-Re, a combination of two deities); Osiris, god of the dead and his sister-wife Isis; Horus, their son (usually depicted with a hawk's head); Ptah, the artificer-god; Khonsu, god of the moon; Mut, the mother-goddess, and so on, there were legions of minor gods and goddesses who were originally local deities worshipped by the tribes who lived along the banks of the Nile in pre-Dynastic times.

We know about these religious beliefs from a number of sources. First there were certain religious texts, commonly known as "The Book of the Dead," copies of which were buried in tombs. A more accurate translation is "The Book of What Is in the Underworld." This book is a bizarre collection of spells and incantations allegedly designed to guide the *ka* (soul) of the dead man through the twelve caverns of the Underworld. The Egyptians appear to have believed that as the sun-god, Re, crossed the sky from east to west during the twelve hours of the day, so he had to return from west to east along a Nile that flowed through twelve caverns under the earth, which of course was flat. These texts, with accompanying sculptured and painted reliefs, adorn the tombs of the pharaohs in the Valley of the Kings' Tombs near Luxor. Here is an extract from one of these texts, which is in the form of question and answer. The soul of the dead monarch had to be ready with the right answers when he was accosted by good and evil spirits he might meet when making his nightly journey in company of the sun-god, Re.

Questioner. Who, pray, art thou? What is thy name?
King.　 "He who groweth under the Grass and dwelleth in the Olive Tree" is my name.
Questioner. Pass on then.
King.　 I pass to the place north of the Olive.
Questioner. And what didst thou see there?

King.	A thigh and a leg.
Questioner.	And what said they to thee?
King.	That I shall see the greetings in the land there of the Fenkhu.
Questioner.	What did they give thee?
King.	A flame of fire and a pillar of crystal.

And so on, ream after ream of it; meaningless gibberish to us, and probably also to the men who copied it from the ancient writings. However, it was a ritual which had to be performed correctly, and ritual, however meaningless, meant much in the life of the ancient Egyptian. These texts were almost certainly a relic of distant days when the prehistoric ancestors of the civilized Egyptians lived along the banks of the fecund Nile and performed magical spells, the original significance of which had long been forgotten when the tombs in the Royal Valley were inscribed—another instance of Egyptian conservatism.

It was different with the nobles and their wives. They did not aspire to be gods. All they hoped for in the afterlife was a continuance of the good things they had enjoyed in life. They hoped to continue to enjoy the same rank, to be able to go on hunting parties on the Nile, to give rich feasts for their friends, to command armies or fleets of ships as they had done on earth. This, incidentally, was why they and their masters the pharaohs took such care to preserve their earthly bodies by mummification and deep interment within protective coffins and sarcophagi. According to ancient Egyptian belief, if the body perished so did the *ka* or spirit which inhabited it.

For at least two thousand years many of the tombs, including the royal ones, have been accessible to visitors. There are records of Greek and Roman tourists who explored them more than eighteen hundred years ago. They, like us, saw on the walls of the nobles' tombs sculptured reliefs or paintings depicting, among other scenes, parties at which men and women in elegant dress listened to musicians or watched dancers, waited on by slaves who served them with rich food and wine. They too were delighted, as we are, by colorful paintings showing noblemen and their wives and pretty daughters hunting wildfowl in the marshes beside the Nile. Sometimes we see a nobleman spearing fish from a light papyrus skiff, while his daughter holds onto his legs to prevent his falling into the water. One can see these same reliefs and paintings today in the Tomb of Tiye at Sakkara or that of Rekhmire in Thebes. But we know, thanks to our ability to read the inscriptions, that a thousand years separate Tiye from Rekhmire, even though the scenes in their tombs are very similar.

We can now also read the writings which accompany these reliefs or paintings and tell us what the people depicted are doing and saying, as in a modern comic strip. On the whole they tend to be monotonous and repetitive, but occasionally the artist has been allowed a little license. In the tomb of Rekhmire, who was prime minister under the pharaoh Tuthmosis III, a lady of the court, holding out her winecup, is represented as saying, "I wish to drink until I am drunk. My inside is like a straw!" And one of the naked girl servants, as she hands a lotus flower to one of the guests, says, "Enjoy a festive day."

In another part of Rekhmire's tomb, which is so elaborately inscribed that a whole book has been devoted to it, some of Rekhmire's duties are outlined:

It is he who hears the case regarding any deficit in the Temple dues. It is he who assesses any assessment in kind

55

for anyone who has to pay one to him. It is he who hears all law cases. It is he who allows reductions in the imposts on places of industry. . . . It is he who opens the House of Gold in connection with the High Treasurer. It is he who inspects the tribute of Byblos. . . . It is he who inspects the water-supply on the first of every ten-day period. . . . He it is who fits out ships according as anyone is fitted for it. He it is who despatches any messenger of the Royal Demesne . . . when the Monarch is on an expedition. . . . Lo, as to the position of Vizier, lo, it is not pleasant at all, no, it is bitter as gall.

Large books have been devoted to the rich treasury of Egyptian literature, though this represents only a tiny portion of what must once have existed. Besides historical chronicles there are works of fiction, letters, legends, school exercise books, proverbs or "wisdom literature," and poetry, including some charming love songs. None of these would have been available to us but for the brilliant efforts of Champollion and other decipherers.

Here are some brief selections from documents, chosen mainly because they reveal the hearts and minds of the ancient Egyptians and show us how close they were, in many ways, to ourselves. First, here is a letter from a widower to his dead wife. The bereaved husband was struck down by an illness, and some witch-doctor or magician had cruelly suggested that the misfortune was due to the sick man's having injured or neglected his wife during her lifetime. Evidently the wife died while the husband was on foreign service. The husband, on the advice of the magician, caused this letter to be placed in her tomb, where it was found by archaeologists:

> What evil have I done to you, that I should find myself in this wretched state? What then have I done to you, that

56

you should lay your hand upon me, when no evil was done to you? You became my wife when I was young, and I was with you. I was appointed to all manner of offices, and I was with you. I did not forsake you or cause your heart any sorrow. . . . Behold, when I commanded the foot-soldiers of Pharaoh, together with the chariot-force, I did cause you to come that they might fall down before you, and they brought all manner of good things to present to you. . . . When you were ill with the sickness which afflicted you, I went to the Chief Physician and he made you your medicine, he did everything that you said he should do. When I had to accompany Pharaoh on his journey to the south, my thoughts were with you, and I spent those eight months without caring to eat or drink. When I returned to Memphis, I besought Pharaoh and betook myself to you, and I greatly mourned for you with the people of my house.

Among the interesting facts revealed by the decipherment is the literal meaning of certain ancient Egyptian proper names. Sir Alan Gardiner has quoted a number of these including the following names for sons: "Riches Come," "His Father Lives," "Chief of the Mercenaries" (obviously a soldier's son). And among girls' names are "Beauty Comes," "Ruler of her Father," and most touching of all, because it obviously refers to the mother having died in childbirth, "Replace Her."

Among the wisdom literature is the following passage by the great sage 'Eney which bears witness to the love and respect which at least some Egyptians afforded their womenfolk:

Thou shalt never forget what thy mother has done for thee. . . . She bare thee and nourished thee in all manner of ways. If thou forgettest her she might blame thee, she might lift up her arms to God and He would hear her

57

complaint. After the appointed months she bare thee, she nursed thee for three years. She brought thee up, and when thou didst enter the school, and wast instructed in the writings, she came daily to thy master with bread and beer from her house.

And another reads:

If thou art a man of note, found for thyself an household, and love thy wife at home, as it beseemeth. Fill her belly, clothe her back, unguent is the remedy for her limbs. Gladden her heart, as long as she lives; she is a goodly field for her lord.

In the tomb paintings are given the names by which husbands addressed their wives, among which are "Loving One," "First Favorite," "My Mistress Is As Gold," and "This Is My Queen." In fact women, certainly among the higher ranks of society, seem to have enjoyed a good life, better than the women of Greece and Rome. All inheritance was through the female line, never through the male. A man could not become a pharaoh except by marrying the heiress, either widow or daughter, of the preceding pharaoh. Again it is through the decipherment of the writings that we have learned this.

In modern Egypt, as in all Arab lands, the reverse is true; male children are always more highly valued than female.

Adoration of female beauty is very obvious from some of the writings; nor was this beauty something necessarily enjoyed in private. A great dancer, for instance, could inspire the homage of thousands, not only of men but of women as well. Here is a very free translation, by the late Arthur Weigall, of a poem in honor of one of the daughters of the reigning pharaoh. It is not a literal translation, but I have chosen it because it conveys so well the sweep and rhythm of the dance. Hearing these lines it is not difficult to imagine the scene: the king and queen seated on their thrones, the courtiers massed around, and the tones of the harps and tambourines as the dancer makes her entrance;

> Sweet of love is the daughter of the King!
> Black are her tresses as the blackness of the night,
> Black as the wine-grapes are the clusters of her hair
> The hearts of the women turn towards her with delight
> Gazing on her beauty with which none can compare.
>
> Sweet of love is the daughter of the King!
> Fair are her arms in the softly-swaying dance,
> Fairer by far is her bosom's rounded swell,
> The hearts of the men are as water at her glance
> Fairer is her beauty than mortal tongue can tell.
>
> Sweet of love is the daughter of the King!
> Rose are her cheeks as the jasper's ruddy hue,
> Rose as the henna which stains her slender hands!
> The heart of the King is filled with love anew,
> When in all her beauty before his throne she stands.

By way of contrast, here is an ancient Egyptian poem more than three thousand years old which conveys the agony of unrequited love as well as anything which has been written since:

> Seven days from yesterday I have not seen
> my beloved.
> And sickness has crept over me,
> And I am become heavy in my limbs
> And am unmindful of my own body.
>
> If the master-physicians come to me
> My heart has no comfort from their remedies,

And the magicians, no resource is in them;
My malady is not diagnosed.

Better for me is my beloved than any remedies,
More important for me than the entire compendium
    of medicine
My salutation is when she enters from without.
When I see her, then am I well;

Opens she her eye, and I am strong;
And when I embrace her, she banishes evil,
And it passes from me for seven days.

7 ❧ THE MYSTERY OF CUNEIFORM

The decipherment of what is known as cuneiform (nail-shaped or wedge-shaped) writing was one of the most painfully difficult tasks ever attempted. It took a very long time, and scores of scholars from many lands contributed to the solution over a period of more than a century and a half. For this and other reasons it is also one of the most difficult linguistic feats to explain in simple terms, more abstruse even than the decipherment of ancient Egyptian.

Most people have seen, at some time or another, examples of cuneiform writing, with its neat wedge-shaped characters, on baked clay tablets in museums, or illustrated in books. It lacks the pictorial appeal of the ancient Egyptian hieroglyphs, but in some ways it is more important and in-

teresting than ancient Egyptian; it was used not by one race
or nation but by numerous peoples throughout western Asia
to write their own languages.

In short, it was not a language in itself, but a system of
writing which could be adapted to many languages, like our
Latin alphabet which can be used equally effectively for
writing in English, German, French, Italian, Spanish, and
other tongues. Its importance lies in the fact that, once deciphered, it enabled scholars to read and translate the literature of the Sumerians of Lower Mesopotamia, who appear
to have invented it; the Semitic Akkadians who lived to the
north of the Sumerians and eventually absorbed them; the
Babylonians and the Assyrians mentioned frequently in the
Old Testament; the Amorites; the people of Ugarit on the
Syrian coast; the Luvians, Hurrians, and Hittites of Asia
Minor; the Old Persians; and other peoples who inhabited
western Asia between ca. 3000 B.C. and later than 400 B.C.
However, the fact that the cuneiform signs were used to
write in so many tongues made them all the more difficult
to decipher.

The story of the decipherment begins in the sixteenth
and seventeenth centuries A.D. with the exploration by a few
adventurous European travelers of the ruins of Persepolis in
Persia (modern Iran). Here, on an artificial terrace forty
miles northeast of Shiraz on the lower slopes of the mountain called Kuh-i-Rahmat, the Persian kings of the Achaemenid Dynasty (550–330 B.C.) built a series of splendid
palaces. From these, at the height of their power, they
ruled an immense empire extending over most of what is
now the Middle East. The names of some of these kings are
familiar from classical history: Cyrus, Darius, Xerxes. It was
Darius I who attempted to invade Europe via Greece in 490
B.C. and was defeated by ten thousand Greeks at the battle

of Marathon. His successor Xerxes, with a much mightier force drawn from the subject peoples of his Empire, launched a combined land and sea attack on Greece in 480 B.C. During the campaign he defeated the Greeks at Thermopylae and took and burned Athens, but he later was defeated at sea at the historic battle of Salamis and on land at the battle of Plataea. If he had won he might have added Europe to his Empire and the whole history of western civilization would have been different.

One hundred and fifty years later, in 330 B.C., the Greeks under their Macedonian leader Alexander the Great wreaked their ultimate revenge. After pursuing and defeating the Persian king Darius III at the battle of Arbela, Alexander took Persepolis, and after a night of drunken revelry set the palaces on fire, urged on, it is said, by his favorite courtesan Thais. The magnificent timberwork of the roof, the splendid furniture and hangings, all were destroyed, but the walls and columns remained, though often ravaged later by plunderers in search of building stone. Incised on some of these walls were inscriptions in what we now recognize as cuneiform writing, but it would appear that even in the time of Herodotus (fifth century B.C.) European visitors to Persepolis could not understand them. Both Herodotus and Strabo speak of "Assyrian characters" and Diodorus calls them "Syrian." Nor is it likely that many of the Persians themselves understood anything but the "Old Persian" form of the inscriptions which we now know were trilingual, that is, they repeated the same message in three different languages.

Besides the Persepolis inscriptions there were other inscribed rocks, for example the sheer cliff of Naksh-i-Rustam opposite the palace of Darius, with its portraits of kings; the rock-cut tombs of Darius I, Xerxes, Artaxerxes, and Darius

The ruins of Persepolis stand on a tremendous platform built from the limestone from the mountain nearby.

II; and about twenty-five miles away the great tomb of Cyrus the Great (559–529 B.C.). These monuments and inscriptions were seen by a handful of European travelers from the fifteenth to the seventeenth centuries, brave and adventurous men like Giosofat Barbaro, who went to Persia in 1472 as representative of the Venetian Republic, Don Garcia de Silva Figueroa, a Spaniard who visited Persepolis in the sixteenth century, and Pietro della Valle, an Italian who, after a disastrous love affair, embarked from Naples in 1614. He went to Turkey, Egypt, Jerusalem, Syria (where he found himself a bride), and thence through Persia to India.

Pietro della Valle was an extraordinary young man. He went to Babylon and brought back inscribed bricks. At Persepolis he mistook the palaces of the Achaemenid kings for temples, but observed the inscriptions carefully and copied some of them. Unlike some other travelers he refused to believe that these wedge-shaped signs were mere decoration, but was convinced that they represented a language; and he even noticed a recurrent series of five symbols which had great significance in the ultimate decipherment. These copies by della Valle were the first examples of cuneiform writing to be brought to Europe.

I have described these early travelers as brave and adventurous because virtually from the defeat of the Crusaders by the Moslems western Asia had been closed to Europeans. Those who ventured into these forbidden lands were exposed not only to the normal hazards of travel, including disease, but also to the hostility of the native peoples, to whom an "infidel" was an object of hatred and contempt. A few men tried to make the journey, impelled by curiosity and a love of adventure, and more than one paid with his life; some died of disease, others were robbed and murdered. Yet still a trickle of bold-spirited travelers essayed the hazardous journey through those then little-known lands.

Among these was a Frenchman named Jean Chardin who made his journeys between 1666 and 1681. When he was twenty-two his father sent him to the East Indies to buy diamonds. He returned via Persia, and although he was not an antiquary or linguist he made remarkably accurate drawings of Persepolis and gave a good description of its inscriptions. In 1681 he settled in London and King Charles II made him a baronet. His *Travels* were published in 1711 with his beautiful drawings. Like Pietro della Valle, he was convinced that the inscriptions represented an unknown language and were not mere decorative motifs. But it was one of his successors, Engelbert Kampfer from Lemgo, Germany, who coined the phrase *litterae cuneatae* (wedge-shaped or nail-shaped writing). Kampfer, too, copied parts of the inscriptions and published them.

But the first great advance towards the decipherment of the cuneiform was made by Carsten Niebuhr, son of a pastor of Holstein in Germany. He was educated at the University of Gottingen where he read Kampfer's works, which made him decide to journey to the Middle East. In 1761 he started out with a Danish expedition headed for Bombay. It was literally a death-march, and every one of the party died from either disease or violence during the journey. Carsten himself only escaped death by disguising himself as a native. By the time Niebuhr reached Bombay he had only one companion among those with whom he had started from Denmark, and that was the doctor of the expedition. The doctor died on board ship and Niebuhr disembarked at Bombay alone.

Nevertheless, he determined to make the return journey via Persia, and in March of the following year, 1762, he caught his first sight of Persepolis. For three weeks he zealously copied the inscriptions, and when he returned to Europe he published them in a book called *Description of a Voyage to Arabia and the Neighbouring Lands* (1774–1778). His were the best copies made up to that date, and his accompanying descriptions were pertinent and astute. He was the first to recognize that at Persepolis there were three sets of inscriptions in three separate languages, and that the relatively few signs in one set of inscriptions pointed to its being alphabetic. He even worked out an alphabet of forty-two characters, of which thirty-two proved to be correct.

Many other travelers, some scholars and others amateurs, were to contribute to the decipherment over the next seventy years, however indirectly. In 1800 it was understood that certain of the Achaemenid kings of Persia mentioned by Herodotus, who used the Greek forms of their names (Hyataspes, Cyrus, Xerxes, Darius), had been commemorated on the walls of Persepolis and in certain rock-cut inscriptions on the cliffs of the Persian mountains. It was also recognized that these inscriptions were trilingual.

Scholars had also accepted the fact that one of these languages was Old Persian and was mainly alphabetic. The second was written in a syllabic script, each symbol standing for a consonant plus a vowel or vice versa (like our own words *be, to, in, at*) or even a vowel and two consonants (like our *bin, rat,* or *man*). This language was probably Elamite. The third script, however, which we now call Babylonian for want of a better word, was much more complicated. It was probably the oldest and most primitive of the three, using far more signs; it used not only phonograms but also pictograms and ideograms, like ancient Egyptian. Yet all three languages were written in the same cuneiform script, differing not in style, as do the Egyptian hieroglyphic, hieratic and demotic writings, but only in the number of characters used and the order in which they were placed.

Also, around the turn of the century, explorers like the Englishman Claudius Rich had begun to find in Babylon baked clay bricks and tablets inscribed in the cuneiform script which was for convenience called Babylonian, though much of it was far older than Babylon. It gradually became clear to philologists that although "Babylonian" was probably the oldest form of this writing system, the key to its decipherment lay in the Old Persian inscriptions current in the time of Darius and Xerxes.

The main trouble was that even if the inscriptions at Persepolis and other sites were in Old Persian, the sound values attributed to the names of the well-known Persian kings of the Achaemenid period would not be their Greek forms, Darius, Xerxes, Artaxerxes, but the way the Old Persians pronounced them. Only if this could be established beyond reasonable doubt could the decipherment progress. It was the same problem which confronted the Egyptian philologists. Some had thought that they could read the hieroglyphs without being able to pronounce them. It was only when such men as Champollion recognized that the ancient language survived partially in the Koptic church ritual that an approximation of the original phonetic values could be estimated, and this assisted their understanding of the grammatical structure of the language.

A young Frenchman named Abraham Hyacinthe Anquetil du Perron (1731–1805) had originally been trained as a theologian but was fascinated by the Zend religion of Old Persia, and set himself to study it in Paris. At this time Orientalism was a cult among European scholars and the subject which most attracted du Perron was the sacred writings of the *Parsees,* survivors of the Old Persians who had emigrated to India from Persia in the face of Moslem persecution. They were sun- and fire-worshippers, and Kampfer had seen two of them kneeling in prayer before the flaming oil gushers of Baku as he passed that way on his travels. They were known to have taken with them certain sacred books in Old Persian including their most holy work, the *Zend Avesta,* and it occurred to du Perron that here might lie the clue to the pronunciation and grammar of the Old Persian inscriptions.

He made a special journey to India to seek out this information. He made himself acceptable to the Parsee priests, the *dasturs,* though he found they could only read these ancient texts in modern Persian. He stayed with the *dasturs* for seven years, after which he returned to France. He brought back not only the original text of the *Zend Avesta* but also a translation into modern Persian which one of the *dasturs,* Darab, had dictated to him letter by letter, a tremendous addition to scholarship that brought the decipherment of the cuneiform writing considerably nearer. This shows the lengths to which scholars went to obtain the information they needed. Although du Perron cannot by any stretch of imagination be called the decipherer of cuneiform, without the information he acquired during that seven-year stay in India it might still remain a mystery.

Other scholars followed in his footsteps, though not all forsook the security of their studies to brave the hardships of travel in Persia. One was Olaus Gerhard Tychsen (1734–1815), a noted Hebrew scholar. In 1798, following Niebuhr, he published a paper on the cuneiform scripts of Persepolis. Unlike Niebuhr he was prepared to attribute phonetic values to the characters. He even tried to discover in groups of signs the composition of certain "words," by comparing the signs with words he already knew from other

Semitic and Indo-European languages. He had scant success, but he made two substantial contributions to the field. He confirmed that the Persepolitan inscriptions represented three separate languages, and he noted a certain sign, an isolated oblique wedge, which he recognized as a division between words.

Another German, Friedrich Munter (1761–1830), agreed with this, and acknowledged that three separate languages were represented in the cuneiform script. He also suggested that the first version was alphabetic (Old Persian), the second syllabic (Elamite), and the third an ideographic form of writing.

In the early part of the nineteenth century the stage was set for a breakthrough. This was achieved mainly by two researchers, a German named Georg Friedrich Grotefend, and a tough, athletic British Army officer named Henry Creswicke Rawlinson whose duties took him to Persia.

8 ✏ GROTEFEND'S BREAK-THROUGH

The decipherment of unknown languages requires not only patience and scholarly discipline, but also considerable imagination. As an example, try to see the following alphabetic symbols as signs of which the meaning is totally unknown. This is not easy to do, but it will help considerably in understanding how first the Old Persian language and later the Babylonian language was deciphered.

(1) P R E S I D E N T   J O H N   K E N N E D Y
(2) W A S   S U C C E E D E D   B Y
(3) P R E S I D E N T   L Y N D O N   J O H N S O N
(4) W H O   W A S   S U C C E E D E D   B Y
(5) P R E S I D E N T   R I C H A R D   N I X O N

Imagine that you do not know the meaning of any of those odd shapes which we call letters of the alphabet. Nevertheless you would have noticed, if you were observant, that the same nine letters occurred at the beginning of lines (1), (3) and (5), so they clearly represent the same word. Now suppose that you are a philologist of 4000 A.D. staring up at these signs cut on a mountainside in, say, Colorado. And suppose you know that in the twentieth century A.D., two thousand years before your time, the United States of America was governed by rulers called *presidents*. Moreover, you know roughly how this word *president* was pronounced, because you had studied other ancient writings in which this word had been preserved. English, one must assume, has passed completely out of use. You could now begin the process which decipherers call "experimental substitution." You could begin by assuming that this word of nine characters which occurred three times in five lines, in the same place relative to the rest of the line, stood for *president*; and you could begin to substitute the phonetic or "sound" values for each of the characters, *p, r, e, s, i, d, e, n, t*.

At this stage you have no idea whether or not you are right; you are just experimenting. But from your reading of ancient history you know that there were three successive presidents of the United States called respectively Kennedy, Johnson, and Nixon. You do not know exactly how their names were pronounced, but you have a vague idea because there still exists, in some remote part of southern California, a group of people who have retained some of the ancient English language in their church rituals. So you set to work as follows:

If *president* really does mean "president" and the two words following it in line (1) mean "John Kennedy" then the sound value *n* which is the eighth character in *president* should also be the third character in *Kennedy*. You look, and are delighted to find that it is, though repeated twice, for some obscure reason. However, let us look at some of the other signs. If the four characters making up the word *John* are sounded exactly like the first syllable of *Johnson*, then characters ten and thirteen in line (1) should be identical to characters sixteen to nineteen in line (3). And sure enough they are! You have established no less than twelve sound values for the characters cut in the rock. Can you go a bit further? Let us see. You know that Kennedy's successor was a man named Lyndon Johnson. You have established the phonetic values of *J*, *o*, *h*, *n* (though *h* presents difficulties since it does not appear to have a sound in this context). If this really does mean "Lyndon Johnson," then the eighth symbol in the word *president* should also occur in the third and sixth symbols of the assumed word *Lyndon*. And it does.

Nor need you stop at this point, because you have another president, Richard Nixon, whose name may occur in line (5) if your theory is correct. Also, if you happened to know that the formulaic phrase between the names was *was succeeded by* or *who was succeeded by*, you would have identified several more characters besides those which already occurred in the names of the presidents. But you might be puzzled by the fact that the symbol *h* in *John* is not sounded, whereas in *who* it is (though the symbol *w* is silent); also that the sound value of *y* in *Lyndon* is the same as that of the character *i* in *Nixon*, whereas in the word *Kennedy* the sound value of the character *y* is *ee*.

The parallel between the efforts of Grotefend and Rawlinson and those of some imaginary philologist living two thousand years hence is, of course, very inexact. The real business of decipherment is much more complex and brain-taxing.

Georg Grotefend was born in 1775 at Munden, Germany. He studied theology and philosophy at Göttingen University, and probably contributed more than any single human being, save Rawlinson, to the decipherment of cuneiform. It has been suggested by some writers that he was essentially a brilliant intuitive amateur whose decision to attempt the decipherment of cuneiform was a result of a bet made during a drinking bout. The story may well be true, but it would be wrong to assume from this that Grotefend was a superficial character. He had made a deep study of classical philology; he was familiar with the works of such classical authors as Strabo, Pliny, and Herodotus, in their original languages. He enjoyed the patronage of distinguished men of letters like Christian Gottlieb Heyne, head university librarian at Göttingen, as well as Olaus Gerhard Tychsen.

Grotefend was a schoolmaster of twenty-seven when he decided to attack the cuneiform problem. He read everything available to him. Though he was not an Oriental scholar he had friends who were, and they helped him, either directly or indirectly. He noticed that both Tychsen and Munter had observed a group of seven signs, repeated twice and followed by a smaller group. Here they are:

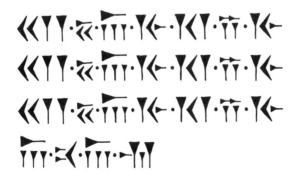

Tychsen had made the mistake of attributing these signs to the period of the Arsacid Dynasty, three centuries after the Achaemenian period, and he tried to identify them with the name of Arsacid kings. ("Arsacid" is from Arsaces I, founder of the kingdom of the Parthians.) But Munter had brought forward evidence that the dynasty to which the inscriptions belonged was that of the Achaemenids—Cyrus, Darius, Xerxes, and the rest—and he argued that in this case "the double grouping of the signs almost certainly stood for the familiar phrase 'King of Kings' . . . in which event the word immediately preceding it must be the monarch's name." But Munter then went astray and the rest of his investigations proved abortive.

Grotefend, however, recognized that Munter was almost certainly right in attributing the Persepolis inscriptions to the Achaemenid Dynasty, and—from his knowledge of classical literature—believed that one of these groups of signs stood for the words *King of Kings*. Picking out two inscriptions from Niebuhr's copies, he noticed that what he supposed to be the *King of Kings* word-group appeared in both, and that the shorter word-group was also used in the first line of the two inscriptions without the presumed phrase *of Kings*. Instead it was followed by another word which Grotefend supposed meant "great," so that one had the phrase *King great* or *great King*.

If his theory was correct then this group of signs would be preceded by a royal name. But what name? Not the same one, because in each of the two inscriptions the opening words were different although the group of signs which followed was the same. To return for a moment to our modern parallel, slightly altered to follow Achaemenid precedent, you might get the following word-groups:

L Y N D O N   J O H N S O N   P R E S I D E N T
R I C H A R D   N I X O N   P R E S I D E N T

You have guessed the meaning of the signs which we
read as *president,* which are identical in both cases. But
who do the preceding signs stand for among the known list
of American presidents? Grotefend had this kind of problem
when tackling the Old Persian alphabetic inscriptions. Of
course he knew the names of the Achaemenid kings in their
Greek forms, Cyrus, Darius, Xerxes, but these were of little
help because the script was not in Greek but Old Persian,
and undoubtedly the Persians would have spelled and pronounced the names of their monarchs differently from the
Greeks.

Grotefend, from his knowledge of the Pehlevi language
(which he had acquired through reading the works of de
Sacy) was able to identify a group of signs which he
guessed meant "son," and it appeared to him highly likely
that the first monarch of the first inscription was the son
of the second monarch in the second inscription. Three
members of the Achaemenid Dynasty appeared to be represented, but the question was, which? He finally decided
by a process of elimination that they could only be:

Darius, Great King, King of Kings . . . son of Hystaspes.
Xerxes, Great King, King of Kings . . . son of King Darius.

This deduction was worked out partly by the fact that
Grotefend knew from classical sources that Hystaspes was
not a king, and his was the only proper name in the inscription which was not preceded by the group of signs to which

77

Grotefend had assigned the meaning "King." There were, therefore, the names of four rulers, three of whom were kings, and two bearing the same name, *Darius*. Even so this was only inspired guesswork, because Grotefend well knew that he could not use the Greek names of these kings in ascertaining the phonetic values of the symbols. He had to find out how the ancient Persians themselves pronounced these royal names. And here he was assisted by the research of du Perron, the Frenchman who had spent seven years in India with the Parsee *dasturs*.

He read the *Zend Avesta* in du Perron's translation and discovered that Hystaspes (the Greek version of the name) could be pronounced *Goshtasp*, *Kistasp*, *Wistasp* or *Gustasp*. He then selected the cuneiform sign which he thought might represent Hystaspes, chose the form *Goshtasp* from the four alternatives available in the *Zend Avesta*, and allotted a sound value to each of the cuneiform signs.

He then argued that if the cuneiform signs which he assumed represented *Darius* really did mean "Darius," only in the Persian version of the word, then some of the signs of the word *Goshtasp* would be repeated in the Persian form of *Darius*. After some experimentation he decided that this form was *Darheush*—the *a* and the *sh* values being common to both names, though in different positions. So eventually he got this:

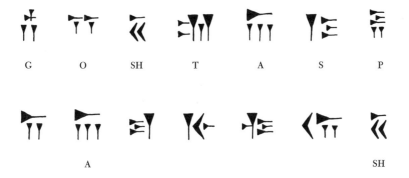

G   O   SH   T   A   S   P

A   SH

Eventually he established the Old Persian pronunciation of *Xerxes* as well, this also containing the *sh, a, h,* and *r* sounds. It is shown here in association with *Goshtasp* and *Dareush.*

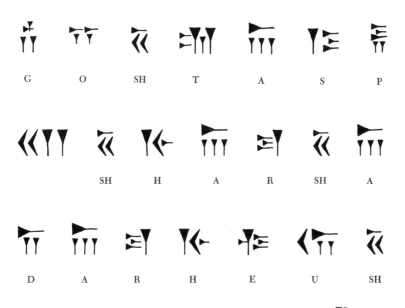

G   O   SH   T   A   S   P

SH   H   A   R   SH   A

D   A   R   H   E   U   SH

In the end it turned out that the correct phonetic pronunciation of Xerxes' name in Old Persian was *kh-sh-y-a-r-sh-a* and that of Darius' was *"Daryavush."*

By 1815, at least fourteen signs had been correctly identified, and of these twelve had been determined by Grotefend. And yet in his lifetime he received very little credit for these findings, which were to lead ultimately to the final decipherment of cuneiform.

9 ☙ RAWLINSON AND THE BEHISTUN ROCK

Other scholars who followed up the work of Grotefend were a Danish professor named Rasmus Christian Rask (1787–1832), the Frenchman Eugene Burnouf (1801–1852), and Christian Lassen (1800–1876) who was part German and part Norwegian. It was Rask who, from his deep understanding of Zend and Pehlevi, proved that the language in which the first three columns of the Achaemenian inscriptions were written was closely allied to Zend, and that the *Zend Avesta* was not, as some critics had suggested, of a date later than these inscriptions. Burnouf at the age of twenty-five worked on the Zend manuscripts which had been brought to France by Anquetil du Perron and made an improved translation. In 1832 he came upon a Sanskrit version of the *Yasna* (part of the *Avesta*) which Persian scholars had translated several hundred years earlier. Subsequent students of the cuneiform writing benefited greatly from his work on this, published two years later under the title *Commentaire sur le Yaçna*.

Christian Lassen was an Oriental scholar who also directed his attention to Zend, and to the Old Persian language in general. He was a friend of Burnouf, whom he had met in Paris, and the two frequently exchanged letters after Lassen had established himself at the University of Bonn. Lassen recalled that Herodotus, in describing Darius' crossing of the Bosphorus when he invaded Scythia, had written as follows:

> When he had looked on the waters of the Black Sea, Darius returned by ship to the bridge, which had been designed by a Samian named Mandrocles. Then, after seeing what he could of the Bosphorus, he had two marble columns erected, on one of which was an inscription in Assyrian characters showing the various nations which were serving in his campaign; the other had a similar inscription in Greek.

These columns had disappeared long ago; indeed Herodotus himself describes their removal. But it occurred to Lassen that if it was a Persian custom to inscribe lists of subject peoples, other inscriptions might have survived in Persia or adjoining lands, among which might be the names of peoples who could be identified and thus provide further clues to the sound values of cuneiform writing. Returning to the Persepolis inscriptions he found a catalogue of twenty-four Persian provinces, and he and Burnouf were able to identify twenty of them. By 1845 only half a dozen of the signs in the first (Old Persian) Persepolitan inscription remained unidentified, a tribute to the combined efforts of scholars from many countries.

However, this was only the beginning. There were, as we have seen, three separate versions of the same statements by the Achaemenian kings, in three separate languages, though all in the same cuneiform writing. The Old Persian inscription, the most recent in date, had largely been translated because elements of the ancient language survived in the holy books of the Zoroastrians, such as the *Zend Avesta*. But the other inscriptions in Babylonian and Elamite, the language spoken by the peoples of Elam, a country lying to the east of Babylonia, had not. Babylonian was the most important because by this time, the middle of the nineteenth century, such pioneers as Claudius Rich, an Englishman, and Paul Emile Botta, an Italian, had begun to find masses of baked clay tablets on southern Mesopotamian sites—far from Persia—inscribed in the same system of "Babylonian" cuneiform. This writing took its name from the fact that such inscriptions were first noted on the site of ancient Babylon.

If only these tablets could be deciphered—and there were thousands of them waiting to be unearthed—what a treasury of archaeological information might be found!

The key to such a decipherment, if it could be accomplished, obviously lay with such trilingual inscriptions as those found at Persepolis and elsewhere. As it happens there is a huge inscription carved on a steep mountainside about twenty miles from Kermanshah in Persia, containing over one thousand lines of cuneiform inscriptions, more than all the others combined. It is known as the Behistun Rock, and the inscriptions are written in the same three languages, Old Persian, Elamite, and Babylonian. It is carved on the

sheer face of a high cliff, about three hundred feet above
the main highway, and is therefore inaccessible except to
good climbers—and even they would need to use ladders
and ropes to reach the highest inscriptions.

In the year 1835 a twenty-five-year-old army officer
named Henry Creswicke Rawlinson sat astride his horse,
staring up at the inscriptions hundreds of feet above him.
He had ridden at a fast pace from Kermanshah, where he
had just been appointed adviser to the shah's brother, and
he was highly excited. For Rawlinson this was the culmina-
tion of an ambition. Eight years earlier, when a boy of seventeen, he had travelled out to Bombay from England to
join the East India Company. On the ship he had met Sir
John Malcolm, a notable Oriental scholar who had just been
appointed governor of Bombay. Malcolm had talked a great
deal about Persia and the cuneiform writing and had so
stirred the boy's interest in Oriental languages that within a
year of his arrival in Bombay he had acquired a fair knowledge of Hindustani, Arabic, and the language of Persia.

Not that there was anything in young Rawlinson which
reminded one of the stereotyped picture of the scholar. He
was extremely athletic, loved sports, was over six feet tall, a
fine horseman, a good shot, and a lover of outdoor exercise.
He had been born at Chadlington Park, a fine Georgian
mansion in Oxfordshire, England, and had the usual education of a son of the landed gentry. At school he had excelled
not only in athletics and sports generally, but also at Latin
and Greek. He soon evinced a love of travel and when the
opportunity came to take up a post with the East India
Company he had eagerly accepted.

Dismounting, he looked for suitable "pitches" in the
rock face and then boldly began the climb, watched anx-
iously by his Persian attendants. At length he reached a nar-

row ledge of rock just below the main Persian text, of which there were four hundred lines. On his left were two hundred and fifty lines in the Elamite language. Right above his head, far beyond his reach, were huge rock-cut bas-reliefs showing a crowned figure, evidently a king, saluting a god who hovered above the group with outstretched wings. Below stood rows of abject bound figures with ropes around their necks, evidently captives taken by the king whose foot rested on one who lay on the ground before him. There were short inscriptions above and below these figures, and to the left of the bas-reliefs a much longer inscription in the Akkadian (or Babylonian) cuneiform.

Rawlinson decided to revisit Behistun whenever his duties permitted, and copy the inscriptions. Whenever he had time he would ride over from Kermanshah, climb to the ledge, and then—notebook in hand—make his careful copies, heedless of the sheer drop of three hundred feet behind him. How he was going to reach the higher, less accessible inscriptions he had not yet worked out, but he was sure that with the aid of ropes, ladders, and cradles, and some help from his Kurdish assistants, he could eventually do this.

Concentrating first on the Persian version of the text, he wondered if it contained other proper names of kings and provinces of the Persian Empire besides those commemorated at Persepolis. Rawlinson had been an eager classical scholar and was naturally familiar with Herodotus in the original Greek. He recalled that the historian, in a famous passage in which Xerxes rebukes his uncle Artabanus, makes the king of Persia say:

If I fail to punish the Athenians, let me be no child of Darius, the son of Hystaspes, the son of Arsames, the son of

85

Ariaramnes, the son of Teispes, the son of Cyrus, the son
of Cambyses, the son of Teipses, the son of Achaemenes!

If this family tree, or part of it, were preserved at Behistun or elsehwere, it might give the clue to other Old Persian characters not yet established.

Rawlinson set to work on his perilous perch, copying
the signs on the Behistun Rock, and then spent all his spare
time studying them. He found the following group of five
signs:

A   R   SH   A

The first four signs were already known, but as the
word thus formed, *a-r-a-sh-a,* clearly referred to the *arsames* of the Greeks, the final sign had to stand for the
sound *m.* Thus the word in Old Persian would be sounded
arsham. Another sign group he detected was the following:

A   R   I   Y   A   R   M

The first group of signs, representing the sounds *a-r-i-
y-a-r-m* and one extra sign, gave the name *ariaramnes* if one
assumed, as one must, that the final sign had the value *n.*

Then there was another word containing no less than
nine characters, as follows:

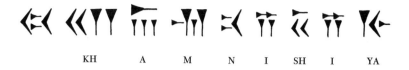

KH   A   M   N   I   SH   I   YA

Rawlinson knew the sound value of all except the first character. Pondering over this word in his study at Kerman- shah he suddenly realized that if he attributed the value *a* to the first sign, he would get the word *a-kh-a-m-n-i-sh-ya*— the word which the Greeks had rendered as *achaemenian*, the very name of the dynasty named after King Achaemenes! The solution to the problem of how two different characters —the first and the third—can have the same value *a* lies in the principle called homophony, which provides that the same sound can be represented by two different signs (com- pare the *i* sound in *Nixon* with the *y* sound in *Lyndon*). The Old Persian name for *Teispes* was also identified as *Tispis*.

The indefatigable young officer worked on until he had completely copied the Old Persian translation and identified numerous other sound values, such as *k* from *katpatuka*, *f* from *Ufraata* (Euphrates), and *b* from *Babirush* (Babylon). When in 1836 he at last heard of the work which Grotefend had done on the Persepolis inscriptions, he realized that the German scholar had little to teach him. Both working inde- pendently had reached many of the same conclusions.

His own descriptions of the difficulties experienced in reaching the inscriptions cannot be bettered:

On reaching the recess which contains the Persian text of the record, ladders are indispensable in order to examine the upper portion of the tablet; and even with ladders there is considerable risk, for the ledge is so narrow, about eighteen inches or at most two feet in breadth, that with a ladder long enough to reach the sculptures sufficient slope

87

cannot be given to enable a person to ascend, and, if the ladder be shortened in order to increase the slope, the upper inscriptions can only be copied by standing on the topmost step of the ladder, with no other support than steadying the body against the rock with the left arm, while the left hand holds the notebook, and the right hand is employed with the pencil. In this position I copied all the upper inscriptions, and the interest of the occupation entirely did away with any sense of danger.

But even greater difficulty attended the copying of the Babylonian inscriptions, which were more important than the Old Persian or Elamite versions of the texts, because by 1847, when Rawlinson made his copies, hundreds of tablets inscribed in the Babylonian system of writing were turning up at such sites as Nineveh in Mesopotamia. Scholars had realized that this was the oldest and most widespread type of cuneiform. Sometimes it is referred to as Akkadian, from the people of Akkad who adopted it from the Sumerians, the original inhabitants of Lower Mesopotamia who appear to have invented this writing system. The Babylonian or Akkadian text was placed so high that, as Rawlinson wrote, "The Babylonian transcript at Behistun . . . can be copied with a good telescope from below, but I long despaired of obtaining a cast of the inscription; for I found it quite beyond my powers of climbing to reach the spot where it was engraved."

Eventually Rawlinson enlisted the help of a "wild Kurdish boy" who "had come from a great distance" and entrusted to him the task of making paper casts of the precious Babylonian texts under the Englishman's supervision. This was in 1847, when Rawlinson had retired from the army and taken a diplomatic post in Baghdad. He writes:

The boy's first move was to squeeze himself into the cleft in the rock a short distance to the left of the projecting mass (of rock). When he had ascended some distance above it, he drove a wooden peg firmly into the cleft, fastened a rope to this, and then endeavoured to swing himself across to another cleft some distance on the other side, but in this he failed, owing to the projection of the rock. It then only remained for him to cross over to the cleft by hanging on with his toes and fingers to the slight inequalities on the bare face of the precipice, and in this he succeeded, passing over a distance of twenty feet of smooth perpendicular rock in a manner which to the looker-on appeared quite miraculous. When he had reached the second cleft the real difficulties were over. He had brought a rope with him attached to the first peg, and now driving in a second, he was enabled to swing himself right over the projecting mass of rock. Here with a short ladder he formed a swinging seat, like a painter's cradle, and fixed upon this seat, he took under my direction a paper cast of the Babylonian translation of the records of Darius.

The stage was now set for the final decipherment of cuneiform in its Akkadian or Babylonian form, a task far more difficult than that of deciphering the Old Persian and Elamite texts, though infinitely more rewarding.

10 ✧ A LOST
WORLD
REVEALED – I

Once copies of Babylonian inscriptions were available for study, especially those copied by Rawlinson from the Behistun Rock, it appeared at first that this language, though written in the same characters as Elamite and Old Persian, was not alphabetic, not syllabic, but partly ideographic; each individual sign could stand for a separate idea.

To illustrate this in modern terms, imagine you had deciphered a script in which the signs *P R E S I D E N T* stood for the sounds making up the word *president*. Then imagine you discovered, in another script using the same characters, that the sign p by itself could stand for *president*, and that *r, e, s,* and the rest could stand for completely different ideas. This is a vast oversimplification, of course, though it contains a partial truth. But the matter was not as simple as that, as Rawlinson and his fellow investigators soon discovered. When inscriptions began to turn up in increasing numbers in Mesopotamia, on such sites as Khorsobad, where Botta was working, Rawlinson directed his attention once again to the Behistun Rock inscriptions. This time he had the firm intention of deciphering the Babylonian version, which bore strong similarities to those being found in the ancient cities of Assyria in Mesopotamia. He knew the general sense of the inscription from the Persian text which he and others had translated; the difficulty was that the Babylonian version of the text consisted of one hundred and twelve lines and over three hundred characters, far more than in the Old Persian or even the Elamite text.

By 1850 Rawlinson had established that the script was not only ideographic. He found out the phonetic values of one hundred and fifty characters and recognized the meanings of about five hundred words by correlation with the Persian text. He had a rival, however, in the shape of a delicate, bespectacled Irish clergyman, the Reverend Edward Hincks, a man who had never been an archaeologist, hardly ever travelled, and worked most of the time at his study desk. In the year when Rawlinson announced despairingly, "I must admit that . . . I was tempted more than once to abandon the study of Assyrian inscriptions because I despaired of ever obtaining a satisfactory result," Hincks stated that in Babylonian, Assyrian, and Akkadian, all differing forms of the same language, there were no single consonants such as *t, l,* or *v.* The signs could be syllabic, made up of a vowel and a consonant like *ab* or a consonant and vowel like *ba,* or they could even combine a vowel and two consonants, like *ban, buk, kan, kap,* or *kub.* Nor was that all. A sign could be polyphonous, having several different sound values. The sign could be sounded *gug, sil, has,* or *kud,* as well as *tar.* Or signs could be homophonous; several different signs could share the same pronunciation. There were nine different signs with the sound value *a.* Or signs could be ideographic, standing for an idea ("king") and not a sound. Rawlinson must sometimes have felt like throwing himself off the Behistun Rock.

And then, even if the correct sound values were established, there remained the question of the language's grammatical structure, the rules by which it was governed and which enabled one to read it. In the case of Old Persian assistance had been given by the *Zend Avesta* and other sacred writings of the Parsees. But what possible relationship did Babylonian-Akkadian-Assyrian have with any known language? Fortunately a very bright Swedish scholar named Isidor Lowenstern established a relationship between ancient Akkadian and modern Semitic languages spoken in western Asia today, such as Hebrew and Arabic. Without these clues it is highly unlikely that this very ancient writing system would ever have been deciphered.

Another problem loomed ever larger as more and more Mesopotamian sites were discovered: Khorsobad, Nimrud, and greatest of all, Nineveh, with the thousands of inscribed tablets that had once formed the royal library of the Assyrian king Ashurbanipal (669–631 B.C.?). The problem arose from the fact that cuneiform writing was very, very old, far older than the Persian Empire, far older than the Assyrians or the Babylonians, older even than the Akkadians. Archaeologists who unearthed these written tablets on many sites confirmed this, and discovered that throughout more than three thousand years the form of writing had changed considerably.

"Moreover," as Professor Cyrus H. Gordon writes, "in

one and the same period different styles of script were used for different purposes. There are also geographical and chronological differences in Sumero-Babylonian writing. A scholar might be perfectly at home in Akkadian cuneiform of the Achaemenian (Persian) period yet unable to recognize the same signs in the earlier and more complicated forms two millennia earlier."

The ancient scribes themselves had been well aware of these difficulties. In Ashurbanipal's great library of tablets at Nineveh, sign lists, grammatical tables, lexicons and other aids to understanding the different forms of the language were discovered. These, when understood, were of great assistance to scholars in unravelling the mysteries of these ancient tongues—Sumerian, Akkadian, Babylonian, Elamite, Hittite, and Persian.

Nevertheless, many scholars, particularly those brought up in the classical disciplines, were sceptical of the ability of the Assyriologists, as they were usually called, since the bulk of the inscriptions had been found in Assyria, to interpret accurately the ancient writings. This matter was put to the test in 1857 when Rawlinson, Hincks, Oppert, and William Henry Fox Talbot were in London at the same time.

In that year the Royal Asiatic Society of London accepted Fox Talbot's suggestion that each of these distinguished scholars be invited to decipher the same script, inscribed on a newly-discovered cylinder of the Assyrian monarch Tiglath Pileser I. Each scholar was instructed to work on the decipherment separately and submit the results in a sealed envelope. When the envelopes were opened the decipherments were found to agree with each other in all but minor details. It now became generally accepted that Babylonian cuneiform, with all its variations, had been deciphered correctly, and a whole new world was opened to the archaeologists of many nations.

Little would be known of Mesopotamian civilization but for the pioneer philologists and archaeologists of the nineteenth century. Mesopotamia is a word of Greek origin meaning "land of the two rivers" or "land between the two rivers," the rivers being the Tigris and the Euphrates. It was in the area to the northwest of the Persian Gulf, alongside and between the two rivers, that one of the two earliest civilizations on earth grew up, the other being that of ancient Egypt.

The reasons for the growth of these two civilizations in Africa and western Asia were basically similar. In each case there were great rivers which, when they flooded, brought down fertile mud on which crops could be grown. In each case wild game lived in the rivers and along their banks. In each case the countries were bounded by inhospitable deserts; the nomadic hunters who had been accustomed to wander from one oasis to the next were induced to settle in a land where they were assured of a continual water supply, fertile soil, and a means of waterborne transport. The main difference is that the flooding of the Tigris and Euphrates is more erratic, and can be more catastrophic, than that of the Nile.

The distinguished Australian archaeologist Gordon Childe suggested that the move towards the rivers probably began as early as about 10,000 B.C., because at this time—the end of the last Ice Age—the climate of this region changed, and the landscape changed from grassland to desert. Naturally, not only human beings, but other animals as well, were forced by the increasing dessication of the land to move towards the great rivers. This enforced proximity of men and animals may have been one cause of what

Childe called "the Neolithic Revolution," during which men who had been hunters learned to tame and domesticate animals, as well as to cultivate wild grasses and eventually produce cereal crops. Thus the main basis of a civilization, the creation of large settled communities, became possible.

The earliest civilization in southern Mesopotamia of which we have knowledge is called "Sumerian." Who the Sumerians were or where they came from has never been established, but no evidence of a civilization earlier than theirs has been found in the land of the Two Rivers. But there was at one time a "King of Sumer and Akkad," and from this we derive the name. Writing can be traced back to the Sumerians as early as 3500 B.C. (though precise dating is hazardous), and in the beginning it was pictographic like early ancient Egyptian, and was used for keeping records. The Sumerians used miniature pictures of birds and other animals, human beings, plants, tools, and buildings to convey a meaning. It was only later that they reduced these pictures to conventional signs which had the same meanings but which were easier to incise on wet clay.

There is a very good reason for this. In Egypt there was an abundance of fine stone on which to carve inscriptions, and also the papyrus plant from which the ancient Egyptians made a durable writing material—the earliest form of paper—on which signs could be written in ink. The Sumerians were not so fortunate. In Lower Mesopotamia there is no stone or papyrus. The most readily accessible material is clay from the river banks, and from this they made their dwellings, temples, shops, and warehouses, and even artificial mountains called *ziggurats*. A ziggurat looked rather like a pyramid, but had a flight of steps leading to the top, on which stood a small temple, the home of the god.

That the Sumerians were the first people to settle in

southern Mesopotamia is indicated by several facts. One is
that on a number of sites archaeologists digging in the ancient mounds marking the locations of cities have found a
clear progression from the earliest levels, where stone implements of the most primitive kind have been found, up
through successive layers where bronze tools and weapons
have been discovered, products of a highly sophisticated
culture capable of erecting large buildings of many types,
from temples and palaces to shops and warehouses.

There can be no doubt that the Sumerians invented
writing even before the ancient Egyptians, who borrowed
several signs from them. The racial origin of the Sumerians
remains obscure, but they were not Semitic, like the Akkadians who occupied the land to the north of Sumer (north of
modern Baghdad) and who absorbed much of their culture.
The Akkadians had to adapt the Sumerian writing system to
their own Semitic language, and clay tablets have been
found on Akkadian sites clearly showing that the early
forms of the language were pictographic. For instance, you
will see in the illustration at the top of the next page Akkadian signs for "star," "sun," "waxing moon" (also standing
for the ideas of "horn" and "to grow"), "eye," "heart," "ox,"
and "fish," which are derived from Sumerian, and which were
eventually stylized as the cuneiform writing system.

The chart at the bottom of the next page shows clearly
how the early pictographic and ideographic script developed
into the cuneiform system.

The signs for "bird," "fish," and "ox" were transformed
into wedge-shaped symbols, easily incised on wet clay
which was afterwards dried in the sun or baked in an oven.
Also, the characters were at one stage turned at an angle of
ninety degrees to make them easier to write from left to
right.

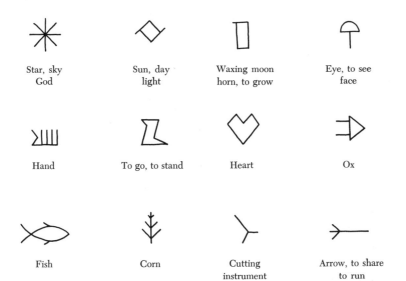

| Star, sky God | Sun, day light | Waxing moon horn, to grow | Eye, to see face |

| Hand | To go, to stand | Heart | Ox |

| Fish | Corn | Cutting instrument | Arrow, to share to run |

MEANING OF SIGN	FIRST POSITION	LATER POSITION	EARLY BABYLONIAN	ASSYRIAN
Bird				
Fish				
Ox				

97

Cuneiform text which describes the siege of Jerusalem by King Sennacherib of Assyria.

Unlike ancient Egypt, the land of Sumer was never completely unified into one kingdom; instead, various city-states grew up with capital cities at such places as Erech, Nippur, and Ur (of the Chaldees, birthplace of Abraham). Although built almost entirely of mud brick, since stone had to be brought from a great distance, these cities were often large and of great magnificence. Their rulers were frequently at war with each other and sometimes one king would gain control of a number of states from which he exacted tribute.

We know about the history of Sumer, Babylonia, and Assyria only from the writings which have survived on monuments, inscribed bricks, and clay tablets which were carefully preserved in royal and temple archives.

In the Assyrian palaces were found magnificent sculptured monuments inscribed in cuneiform, for Assyria was situated where an abundance of fine stone was accessible. Many of these sculptured reliefs were removed from the sites; some are now in the British Museum, some in the Louvre in Paris, and some in the United States. On them the Assyrian monarchs inscribed the records of their wars and conquests, which are valuable historical documents only available since the decipherment of the writing system.

Among the great kings of Babylon and Assyria who left such records are Sargon II (722–705 B.C.), the Sargon of the Old Testament, founder of the last dynasty of Assyria. It was Sargon who made the northern kingdom of Palestine an Assyrian dependency, with King Hezekiah paying tribute. Then there was Sennacherib (705–681 B.C.) who laid siege to Jerusalem and whose army was smitten by the plague, as described in the Bible. To quote Lord Byron's poem:

99

The Assyrian came down like a wolf on the fold
And his cohorts were gleaming in purple and gold
And the sheen of his spears was like stars on the sea
Where the blue wave rolls nightly on deep Galilee.

Sennacherib's palace at Nineveh was excavated in the nineteenth century and many inscribed sculptured reliefs were found. In this case as in others the Assyrian records supplemented and confirmed the Old Testament records. The same is true of the great Babylonian king Nebuchad-nezzar (605–562 B.C.) who ruled the Neo-Babylonian king-dom. It was he who conquered Jerusalem in 598 B.C., taking King Jehoichin to Babylon as prisoner and installing a new monarch, Zedekiah, in Jerusalem. This was the time of the "Babylonian captivity" described in the Jewish chronicles. Finally Babylon was conquered by the Medes and the Per-sians, and under the Achaemenid kings Babylonia became a province of the Persian Empire. But fortunately, as we have seen, the Persian kings continued to use the Akkadian lan-guage on their inscriptions, alongside their own Old Persian script, and it was this which provided Grotefend, Rawlin-son, Hincks, and other scholars with a clue to its ultimate decipherment.

11 ❧ A LOST WORLD REVEALED - II

Consternation over Adad reaches to the heavens
Turning to blackness all that has been light.
The wide (land) is shattered like (a pot)
For one day the south-storm (blew)
Gathering speed as it blew, submerging the mountains,
Overtaking the people like a battle.
No one can see his fellow,
Nor can the people be from heaven. . . .
Man of Shurrupak, son of Ubar Tutu,
Tear down this house, build a ship!
Give up possessions, and seek thou life!
Despise property and keep the soul alive!
Aboard the ship take thou the seed of living things.
The ship that thou shalt build

> Her dimensions shalt be to measure
> Equal shall be her width and her length
> Like the Apsu shalt thou seal her.

That extract is from one of the oldest epic poems in the world, perhaps the oldest: the Story of Gilgamesh, which probably dates from about 3000 B.C. in its original version. The version of which this is a modern translation was found in the royal library of the Assyrian king Ashurbanipal, but other, earlier examples have been discovered. The resemblance of this to the story of Noah's Flood in the Book of Genesis is so striking (and there are other parallels) as to leave no doubt that the Hebrew version was derived ultimately from the Sumerian original, particularly as the wide flat land of Sumeria on the Tigris and Euphrates was and is subject to violent, catastrophic floods, whereas Palestine and Jordan which are upland countries are not. But some of the ancestors of the Biblical Hebrews came from lower Mesopotamia, including Abraham himself, who was born at Ur. They must have brought this story with them. In fact the whole story of the Creation embodied in Genesis bears a striking similarity to that found in Sumerian literature.

The story of the discovery of this historic document is one of the romances of archaeology. It centers around a young man named George Smith (1840–1876), who had been apprenticed as an engraver of banknotes in London. He loved the Bible, and read every work of Oriental literature he could get hold of. Eventually his frequent visits to the British Museum, where he spent days poring over the newly-discovered cuneiform tablets, brought him to the attention of the Museum authorities. One of them, Mr. Samuel Birch, decided to employ him as a restorer. Young George Smith carefully put together the broken fragments of tablets and in a remarkably short time taught himself to read them. In 1866, at the age of twenty-six, he became Assistant Keeper of Oriental Antiquities.

When he was working on the Nineveh tablets in 1872 he came upon a document which was unlike any of the others. It was not a code of laws, or a record of some business transaction, or a list of kings or gods. This was a story, an epic poem about heroes, written with such vigor and sweeping attack that it might be compared with Homer. Its hero, Gilgamesh, part human and part divine, built the walls of Uruk, the capital city of Sumer. The gods, displeased with Gilgamesh, sent a half-human creature covered with hair named Enkidu to attack him. The two fought; Gilgamesh was victorious, and thereafter he and Enkidu became friends. Together they fought against the great Humbaba, god of the cedar forests, and defeated him. The goddess Ishtar (the Sumerian Venus) sent a bull-monster to torment them but in this fight too they were triumphant. The story is full of energy and violent activity, until suddenly Enkidu dies of illness. Then it takes a quieter, more philosophical turn, in which Gilgamesh, now alone, goes on a long journey in search of the secret of life. He knows, says the saga, that the only man who can tell him this is Ut-na-pish-tim, the only survivor of the Great Flood. It was at this point that George Smith suddenly sat up. The Great Flood . . . the Deluge . . . could not this be the same story as told in Genesis, though far earlier? Eagerly he read the tablets and found that the first part of the story was there but just when it reached the account of the Deluge the tablet was broken. Did the missing fragments still exist? The London *Daily Telegraph*, which had whipped up the curiosity of its readers, offered £1,000 to send Smith to Nineveh in search of the missing tablet.

Smith, a timid London scholar unaccustomed to travel,

fearful of the Middle East and the "natives," made the journey, visited Nineveh and searched diligently among the piles of broken fragments. In May 1873 he found the missing seventeen lines of the cuneiform inscription.

> Then the gods led by the evil Enlil took counsel. They would destroy the whole human race to punish it for its countless misdeeds. But Ea, well disposed towards man, sent a dream to his protege Ut-na-pish-tim, revealing the threat which hung over the world. He was ordered to build a boat for himself and his family, the pilot and "the seeds of life of all species." Pious Ut-na-pish-tim obeyed. Then the sluices of the sky were opened and everything human was transformed into mud. But Ut-na-pish-tim's boat drifted for six days and seven nights on the swollen waters until they started to subside, leaving the Ark on the top of Mount Nisir.

The parallel with the Old Testament story is quite striking. When the boat grounds on Mount Nisir Ut-na-pish-tim sends out a dove and a swallow but neither finds a place to settle. After seven days more he sends out a raven which does not return. Then, and only then, does Ut-na-pish-tim leave the Ark and make a rich sacrifice to appease the wrathful gods.

Smith made a third expedition in 1876, during which his companion Ennenberg died of cholera in Aleppo. But Smith went on; he returned to London where, working with Rawlinson, he examined a large clay cylinder with an extensive text. Suddenly he raised his head and declaimed, "I am the first man to read this text after two thousand years." He began to stride about the room, and, according to one version of the story, attempted to take his clothes off, so high was the state of his excitement. Again he was sent out to the

Middle East, to Syria this time, but fell seriously ill. On August 12, 1876, he entered in his diary:

> I'm not well. If we had a doctor here I'm sure I should be all right. But he hasn't come. I am seriously ill. If I die, farewell. . . . I've devoted all my efforts to my scientific studies. I hope that my friends will look after my family. . . . I've carried out my duties to the last. . . .

Six days later Smith died at Aleppo, in the house of the British consul, at the age of thirty-six.

Archaeologists like the late Sir Leonard Woolley have found evidence proving that in Sumer there were many great floods, marked by layers of clean silt containing no evidence of human occupation, although above and below these layers there is such evidence. It is not surprising, therefore, that the biblical Flood story should have its origin in Sumer. Irrigation, the digging of deep canals to carry away the water, was possibly even more important in Sumer than in Egypt. We find evidence of this in a more mundane kind of literature concerned with the proper maintenance of land, and the laws which were drawn up to ensure that this was done. Here are some of the laws taken from the famous Law Code of Hammurabi:

> If a seignior let his field to a tenant, and has already received the rent of the field (and) later Adad (the storm-god) has inundated his field or a flood has ravaged it, the loss shall be the tenant's.

Some of the laws relate to building contractors, who would have envied their modern successors, as sometimes the penalty for inefficient construction meant the loss of the contractor's life.

> If a builder constructed a house for a seignior, but he did
> not make his work strong, with the result that the house
> which he built collapsed and so has caused the death of
> the owner of the house, the builder shall be put to death.

A number of the laws in the Code of Hammurabi concern women, and women's rights in marriage. For example:

> If a woman so hated her husband that she has declared
> "You may not have me," her record shall be investigated
> by the city council, and if she was careful and not at fault,
> even though her husband has been going about and dis-
> paraging her greatly, that woman, without incurring any
> blame at all, may take her dowry and go off to her father's
> house.

But other laws could be harsher:

> If a seignior's wife has brought about the death of her hus-
> band because of another man, they shall impale that
> woman on stakes.

Much Sumerian literature, of course, is religious, concerned with the worship of the gods and goddesses who
ruled the lives of the people. It is important to remember
that to the Sumerians and other ancient peoples religion
was not something set apart from daily life. Nor was it as
concerned with moral duties as Christianity or Buddhism. It
was mainly a matter of propitiating the unseen forces which
governed men's lives: the earth itself, usually imagined as a
woman, because a woman gives birth as the earth gives
birth to plants and animals; the power of the storm, in
Sumer embodied in the fearful storm-god Adad; the god of
the sky Enlil, Inanna, the moon-goddess, and so on.

Some of the hymns to these deities are beautifully com-
posed and very moving. This one, for instance, is addressed to

Ishtar, goddess of love; she was actually a Babylonian deity,
but she had her Sumerian predecessors.

> Praise the goddess, the most awesome of the goddesses.
> Let one revere the mistress of the people, the greatest
> of the Igigi.
> Let one revere the queen of women, the greatest of the
> Igigi.

> She is clothed with pleasure and love.
> She is laden with vitality, charm, and voluptuousness.
> Ishtar is clothed with pleasure and love.
> She is laden with vitality, charm, and voluptuousness.

> In lips she is sweet; life is in her mouth.
> At her appearance rejoicing becomes full.
> She is glorious; veils are thrown over her head.
> Her figure is beautiful; her eyes are brilliant.

> The goddess—with her there is counsel,
> The fate of everything she holds in her hand.
> At her glance there is created joy,
> Power, magnificence, the protecting deity and guardian
> spirit.

In general there is very little of the violent and bar-
baric in Sumerian literature. There are records of wars and
conquests in which one king claims to have subdued the
city-states of his neighbors, but these are rather formal accounts containing little that is bloodthirsty. When we come
to the literature of the Assyrians, whose records were inscribed not only on clay tablets but on the walls of the
kings' palaces, it is very different. The Assyrian sculpture
which adorned these palaces is superb in its vigor and ag-
gressiveness, and the inscriptions describing the kings' conquests seem designed to instill terror and awe in the hearts

of spectators. If we had not already recognized this from Biblical accounts we could tell from the cuneiform inscriptions what a warlike people the Assyrians were and how much they exulted in power.

In one Assyrian relief found at Nimrud by Sir Henry Layard, prisoners of war are shown being impaled on stakes or flayed alive, and the accompanying cuneiform inscription reads:

> I slew one of every two. I built a wall before the great gates of the city; I flayed the chief men of the rebels, and I covered the wall with their skins. Some of them were enclosed alive within the bricks of the wall, some of them were crucified with stakes along the wall; I caused a great multitude of them to be flayed in my presence, and I covered the wall with their skins.

No wonder that when the Assyrians were finally overthrown the prophet Nahum exulted at the thought of their downfall.

> Woe to the bloody city! It is all full of lies and robbery; the prey departeth not.
>
> The noise of the whip, and the noise of the rattling wheels, and the prancing horses, and the jumping chariots. . . .
>
> Thy shepherds slumber, O King of Assyria; they thy nobles shall dwell in the dust; thy people are scattered upon the mountains, and no man gathereth them.
>
> There is no healing of thy bruise; thy wound is grievous; all that hear the bruit of thee clap their hands over thee; for upon whom hath not thy wickedness passed continually?

One of the most interesting aspects of cuneiform decipherment is the manner in which the Assyrian, Babylonian, Akkadian, and Sumerian chronicles confirm or amplify those of the Old Testament. For instance, we read in the Bible of how the Assyrians laid siege to the Hebrew city of Lachish. On an Assyrian bas-relief we can see depicted this very siege; the cuneiform inscriptions verify the Biblical account, and add more detail. Similarly, we know that the Assyrian monarch Sennacherib, in the fourteenth year of the Judean king Hezekiah, "came up against all the fenced cities of Judah and took them."

> And Hezekiah king of Judah sent to the king of Assyria to Lachish, saying; I have offended; return from me; that which thou puttest on me I will bear. And the king of Assyria appointed unto Hezekiah king of Judah three hundred talents of silver and thirty talents of gold. . . .
>
> At that time did Hezekiah cut off the gold from the doors of the temple of the Lord and from the pillars which Hezekiah the king of Judah had overlaid, and gave it to the king of Assyria.

So says the Book of Kings (chapter 19), and this is confirmed by inscriptions found in Sennacherib's palace at Nineveh. Again and again the historical truth of the Biblical chronicles was established by parallel passages in the cuneiform inscriptions of Babylonia and Assyria. This has proved of great help to Biblical scholarship.

In the end, however, after having read the inscriptions of the Assyrians, Babylonians, and Persians and compared their chronicles with those of the Bible, one is drawn inevitably to the writings of that earliest of all Mesopotamian civilizations, Sumer. One does not find Sumerians as attractive physically as the ancient Egyptians. The statues which have survived are strange and somewhat repellent; men and gods are depicted with potbellies and large staring eyes, though this may have been just an artistic convention. It is in their

writings, and not their art and artifacts, that the Sumerians
appeal to us the most.

They lived in large cities, as most of us do today (Ur
had over a million inhabitants); they were burdened, as we
are, by a complex administrative system, and complained
bitterly about taxation. They traded widely; among them
were keen businessmen who lent capital at interest and became very rich. Others remained very poor, and it is of this
fact that a Sumerian poet complains in the following lines:

> Prized is the word of the mighty man who has learned
>   to kill.
> While the weak who have not sinned are humbled.
> Persecuted is the upright man who obeys God,
> The evil man honored and his crimes condoned.
> Riches are heaped upon the rich,
> The goods are filched from a starving man.
> Power is the portion of the victor,
> The weak are flogged and crushed.
> I, too, who am weak, am persecuted by the rich.

Here, as a complete contrast, is a schoolboy exercise in
the form of a dialogue between master and pupil:

MASTER Schoolboy, where did you go from the earliest
        days?
PUPIL   I went to school.
MASTER What did you do in school?
PUPIL   I recited my tablet, ate my lunch, prepared my
        (new) tablet, wrote it, finished it; and then they
        assigned me my oral work, and in the afternoon
        they assigned me my written work. When
        school was dismissed, I went home, and found
        my father sitting there. I told my father of my
        written work, and recited my tablet to him, and
        my father was delighted. . . .

110

Later the master is invited to a good dinner at the house of his pupil's father, probably at the suggestion of the schoolboy, who may not have been as much in favor as his self-approving account suggests. Afterwards the master says:

> Young man, because you did not neglect my word, did not forsake it, may you reach the pinnacle of the scribal art, may you achieve it completely. . . . Of your brothers may you be their leader, of your friends may you be their chief, may you rank the highest of the schoolboys. . . . You have carried out well the school's activities, you have become a man of learning.

All this is reminiscent of the ancient Egyptian scribal literature, for the two societies were similar in many ways. Both were primarily agricultural, and both were dependent on efficient irrigation, as this Sumerian example shows:

> When you are about to cultivate your field, take care to open the irrigation works (so that) their water does not rise too high in it (the field). When you have emptied it of water, watch the field's wet ground so it stays even; let no wandering ox trample it. . . .

Much of Sumerian writing is like this, practical advice to a hard-working, hard-headed, practical people, among whom one would have thought that there was little time left for reflection. And yet, among the "wisdom literature," one finds little philosophical gems which make one feel very close to those ancient people who lived along the Tigris and Euphrates more than five thousand years ago. Here are four which are appealing:

> Who possesses much silver may be happy,
> Who possesses much barley may be happy,
> But he who has nothing at all can sleep.

111

Reading the Past

A restless woman in the house
Adds ache to pain.

For his pleasure: marriage.
On his thinking it over: divorce.

You can have a King, and you can have a Lord,
But the man to fear is the tax-collector.

12 ∾ A SCHOOLBOY
DECIDES

The stories of the decipherment of hieroglyphic and cuneiform writing go back well over a century. But one goes back only to 1954, and as it happens its hero, the late Michael Ventris, was known to me personally. Ventris was about thirty when I first met him in 1954: a slim, fair young man of medium height with firm but sensitive features, a robust jaw, a humorous mouth, and a delightful, self-mocking sense of humor. He was not an archaeologist. He was not even a scholar in the conventional sense; his Classics teacher said that his Greek was "about average," also that he liked sports and was a good Rugby football player. He was by profession an architect.

Ventris was born in the village of Wheathampstead,

some twenty miles from London, in July 1922. His father
was an army officer; his beautiful and talented mother stimulated her son's aesthetic interests and encouraged him to
travel widely in Europe. He had the usual education of a
boy of the upper middle class at that time, a preparatory
school followed by an excellent private school, Stowe. When
he was only fourteen years old a seemingly casual incident
occurred; it set his feet on the path that led to his scaling
what one scholar described as the "Everest of Greek
archaeology"—the decipherment of Cretan Linear B.

What is Linear B? For more than forty years, from the
late eighteen-nineties to the nineteen-thirties, Sir Arthur
Evans had devoted himself to the task of excavating and
partially restoring the great Minoan palace at Knossos in
Crete. He called it, and the civilization it represented, Minoan, after the legendary King Minos with whom it was as-
sociated in classical literature. Homer had written:

> Out in the deep, dark sea there lies a land called Crete, a
> rich and lovely land, washed by the seas on every side and
> boasting ninety cities. One of these cities is called Knossos,
> and there King Minos ruled, and enjoyed the friendship of
> almighty Zeus.

Shortly after Evans had discovered the Palace of Knossos he wrote the following to the London *Times:*

> ". . . the realms of the legendary Minos, the great con-
> queror and lawgiver who at the close of his temporal reign
> took his seat on the dread tribunal of the netherworld, the
> abode of Daedalus, the father of architecture and the plas-
> tic arts, the haunt of the mysterious Dactyls, the earliest
> artificers in iron and bronze, the refuge of Europa, and the
> birthplace of Zeus himself, Crete was in remote times the
> home of a highly developed culture which vanished before
> the dawn of history . . . among the prehistoric cities of

Crete, Knossos, the capital of Minos, is indicated by legend as holding the foremost place. Here the great lawgiver (Minos) promulgated his famous institutions, which like those of Moses and Numa Pompilius were derived from a divine source; here was established . . . a maritime empire, suppressing piracy, conquering the islands of the Archipelago, and imposing a tribute on subjected Athens. Here Daedalus constructed the Labyrinth, the den of the Minotaur, and fashioned the wings—perhaps the sails— with which he and Icarus took flight over the Aegaean.

Although the palace of Minos was an historical fact (Evans dated the earliest occupation to about 3000 B.C. and the first palace to around 2000 B.C.), the stories attached to it were mainly legendary, unlike the chronicles of ancient Egypt, Babylonia, Assyria, and the Hebrew peoples. The reference to Minos' establishment of a maritime empire and suppression of piracy is derived from a short passage in the works of the Greek historian Thucydides. The references to Daedalus, the Dactyls, and the Minotaur come from the works of poets who were repeating folk-myths, probably passed on by word of mouth. Apart from the quotation from Thucydides, there was hardly anything which a modern scientific historian would regard as reliable evidence.

It was this which made Evans's achievement so extraordinary; he had no historical records to guide him, but only myths and traditions. The same was true of his great German predecessor Heinrich Schliemann, who, in the eighteen-seventies, had unearthed a real city of Troy—in fact seven successive cities—and a real Homeric citadel at Mycenae, which Homer described as the home of King Agamemnon, who led the Greek armies to the siege of Troy. Schliemann had been guided only by references in the poems of Homer (written in the eighth century B.C.) which most scholars of that period regarded as pure folk tales.

In fact, until Schliemann's discoveries revealed that a high civilization had existed on the Greek mainland as early as 1700 B.C., classical historians had believed that the history of Greek civilization could be dated not earlier than the first recorded Olympic games (Olympiad) in 776 B.C. Everything that was supposed to be of an earlier date, such as the Trojan War, was dismissed as legend, without historical foundation. But Homer had applied to Mycenae the epithet "rich in gold," and sure enough, when Schliemann excavated the shaft-graves within the citadel he found the bodies of men and women richly adorned with gold. Homer had described in some detail the type of palaces in which his heroes lived and the kind of furniture they had used. At Mycenae, Tiryns, and elsewhere, Schliemann and his successors discovered palaces and remains of furniture closely resembling those which the poet had described. So a new name, *Mycenaean,* was coined to describe the great civilization which had begun on the Greek mainland over a thousand years before the date of the first recorded Olympiad.

Most classical scholars were astonished by this revelation. What they had considered to be legend turned out to contain a kernel of truth. Sir Arthur Evans, who belonged to a generation later than Schliemann's, could not accept the German archaeologist's naive belief that the buildings and objects he had found belonged to the time of Homer, between 800 and 700 B.C. He rightly believed that they belonged to a civilization far older than Homer's time, from which the poet had inherited legends and traditions, presumably passed on by word of mouth through generations of bards.

No literature of this Mycenaean period had ever been found, so it was presumed that the Mycenaeans had not invented writing. Yet, argued Evans, since both ancient Egypt and Sumeria had writing systems at least fifteen hundred years before the building of the first Mycenaean palaces in 1700 B.C., it seemed unlikely that such a highly civilized people as the Mycenaeans could have been illiterate. He had observed on certain "bead-seals" sold by antiquity-dealers in Athens little squiggles which he believed to be writing. He pointed these out to his friend John Myres, a student archaeologist who could make nothing of them. But Evans, who was extremely nearsighted, could, when he held an object close to his eyes, see details with almost microscopic precision. He turned to the antiquity-dealer and asked where these seals had been found.

"In Crete, Mr. Evans," replied the dealer, "in Crete. The country-women there wear them as charms when they are suckling their children. They call them 'milk-stones.'"

Evans and Myres sailed to Crete and began a series of journeys on horseback into the remotest interior of that beautiful, mountainous island. Everywhere they found evidences of ancient buildings, roads, and bridges which reminded them of the "Mycenaean" ruins they had seen on the mainland, though there was a difference. At Knossos, which still bore its Homeric name, and at Phaestos and Mallia, they found evidences of occupation in the form of great mounds which might indicate the presence of buried buildings. They found traditions, too, among the country people; they were told that Mount Juktas, which dominates the landscape around Herakleion, the principal port, was the legendary tomb of Zeus, king of gods, and that the silhouette of the mountain, seen from certain directions, represents the face of the dead or dying god; and that in a cave on Mount Lasithi Zeus had been born to his mother Rhea. Evans found in many a village bead-seals like those he had first seen in Athens, each tiny plaque or cylinder inscribed with pictures and what appeared to be writing, and each bored through the center so it could be worn on the wrist or around the neck. These seals, which the peasant women of Crete wore as charms, were dug up when the men ploughed the land near ancient settlements.

Evans was more than ever convinced that writing had been known to the ancient Cretans, and probably the Mycenaeans too. He determined to excavate a major site in Crete and chose Knossos, a few miles from Herakleion. He hoped to find baked clay tablets like those that had been discovered in such abundance at such Mesopotamian sites as Nineveh and Nimrud. He chose Knossos because it had been mentioned by Homer as the capital of King Minos, and because there on the side of a valley was a great mound, the Mound of Kephala, covering several acres. It also happened that a Cretan archaeologist, appropriately named Minos, had dug some trial pits there and found a number of huge storage jars called *pithoi.*

Digging into the mound, Evans was rapidly rewarded by finding a huge complex of stone buildings, the foundations of which had survived. The arrangement of the numerous rooms and corridors did not follow the typical Mycenaean plan, but among the objects found were many of a Mycenaean type similar to those discovered by Schliemann. The plan of the great palace, which covered over twelve acres, was truly labyrinthine, recalling the myth of Theseus and the Labyrinth. And its foundations date from as early as 2500 B.C., though there were signs of human occupation from five hundred years before that.

The myth of Theseus and the Labyrinth tells us that King Minos, having subdued Athens, demanded as tribute seven virgins and seven young men of good birth, to be sacrificed annually to the Minotaur. This was a monster, half bull and half man, which was kept in a labyrinth under the palace of Minos. Those who were put into the labyrinth never found their way out again, so complex was its maze of dark corridors, and they were slain by the Minotaur.

It happened that in one year Prince Theseus, son of King Aegeus of Athens, volunteered to go to Crete as one of the seven youths. On arrival he was seen by King Minos' beautiful daughter, Ariadne, who fell in love with him. The Greek writer Apollodorus tells us:

> . . . . she gave Theseus a clue (of thread) when he went in. Theseus fastened it to the door, and, drawing it after him, entered in. And after having found the Minotaur in the last part of the labyrinth he killed him by smiting him with his fists; and, drawing the clue after him made his way out again. And by night he arrived with Ariadne and the children (presumably the rest of the Athenian youths and girls destined for sacrifice) at Naxos. There Dionysus fell in love with Ariadne and carried her off.

That is one version of the story. The other, which is probably the true story, states that Theseus deserted Ariadne. The amazing fact is that when Evans dug down into the mound of Kephala he found, still surviving on some of the plastered walls, vividly colored frescoes depicting young men and women leaping over the back of a charging bull. He also found ivory figurines of these "bull-leapers," and, not only at Knossos but elsewhere in Crete, clay figures depicting bulls, in some cases with athletic young men grasping their horns or sitting between them. On the mainland of Greece other objects were found such as the famous

Vapheio cups in which wild bulls are shown being trapped
in nets. Moreover, some of the trappers were women, as
Evans describes:

> The figure on the Vapheio Cup, thus desperately at grips
> with the horns of the great beast, is certainly that of a girl,
> in spite of the sinewy limbs it displays.

The presence of both young men and girls in the bull-
leaping and bull-catching scenes links them directly with
the legend of Theseus and the Minotaur. As for the smith
Daedalus, the splendid though complicated architecture of
the Palace of Minos itself, with its smooth pavements of
polished white gypsum, its pillared halls and corridors, its
many-columned staircases leading to the Royal Apartments,
all point to architectural genius.

On the northeastern side of the palace were many small
rooms which had evidently been occupied by clerks and
artisans. First in this area, and then in other parts of the
palace, Evans found what he came to seek: large numbers
of clay tablets, some rectangular, some shaped rather like
palm leaves, all inscribed with a system of writing which
bore some relationship to what he had noticed on the bead-
seals, but belonged to no known system. It was not hieroglyphic; it certainly was not cuneiform; it was something
quite unique, Europe's earliest known system of writing.
The tablets were provisionally dated to the destruction of
the palace in about 1400 B.C.

There was world-wide excitement among scholars
when this discovery was announced in about 1900. Here, it
was thought, might be found the original literature of the
Greek prehistoric period, literature of which only fragments
had been passed on by oral tradition. However, though
Evans could not read the writing, he soon realized that

*Inscription from the northern entrance passage of
Knossos (top); one from the "Arsenal" at Knossos (bottom).*

these tablets represented lists or inventories of some kind.
The script itself appeared to be syllabic from the number of
separate signs, too many to be alphabetic and too few to be
ideographic. But he noticed that alongside some of the lines
were pictographs representing men, women, chariots, and
swords, together with what he took to be numerals: so many
men, so many women, so many swords and chariots. He also
recognized that some of the tablets were inscribed in one
language, others in another language, though both used the
same script. It was as if some future archaeologist had discovered two books, one in English and one in French, neither of which he could understand, but both in the Latin alphabet. Evans called these two languages Linear A and
Linear B, and at Knossos there were far more inscriptions in
the latter than in the former.

Throughout the forty-odd years during which Evans
worked at Knossos, and other archaeologists, following his
lead, excavated Minoan palaces at Phaestos, Hagia Triadha,
and Mallia, neither he nor any other investigator succeeded
in deciphering either of those scripts. Why not, since the

121

Egyptian hieroglyphs and the Babylonian cuneiform had both been deciphered? The main difficulty was the lack of any bilingual clue, an identical message written in two languages, one known, the other unknown, as in the case of the Rosetta Stone, the Behistun Rock, and the Persepolitan inscriptions. Nothing of the kind turned up in Crete. A single simple bill of lading written by some merchant in Linear A (or Linear B) and Babylonian cuneiform, for instance, would have helped enormously, but nothing of the kind has ever been found, either in Crete or elsewhere. And since both Linear A and Linear B were assumed to be dead languages, the problem seemed insoluble.

Such was the position when Sir Arthur Evans, having been knighted for his achievements at Knossos, gave a talk in the Lecture Hall of the Society of Antiquaries, Burlington House, London, in 1936. He exhibited some of the most precious finds made at Knossos, enthralling his audience with the account of his work there. When the lecture was over and the audience eagerly gathered around the tables where the exhibits were displayed, he moved among them, chatting and discussing their significance. On one table lay a number of Linear A and Linear B tablets, and a group of senior boys from Stowe School were examining them. Among them was a boy who was not even in the Sixth Form (where the average age is seventeen or eighteen). Michael Ventris had managed to tag along with the party when he heard they were going to hear Evans.

The great archaeologist was then eighty-five years of age. The fourteen-year-old boy approached him diffidently and asked, "You said in your lecture, Sir, that the tablets have never been deciphered. Why is that?" Evans explained in detail the difficulties which decipherers had been up against: the great age of the script, the fact that it appeared to be related to no known language, the fact that there was no bilingual clue. Ventris listened carefully. He had already, at the age of eleven, interested himself in the story of the hieroglyphic and cuneiform systems. He thanked Sir Arthur for his explanation. But as the train chugged its way back towards Stowe, Michael was making up his mind. He was going to decipher the ancient Cretan writing system, if it took him a lifetime to do it.

13 ～ THE
MYSTERY
DEEPENS

Of course Michael Ventris was not the only one who decided to struggle with the problems of the Cretan syllabary.
Scholars of various nationalities had been racking their
brains over it for years. It was one of the great challenges of
Greek archaeology. Evans had published copies of the script
under the title *Scripta Minoa* in 1909, and had even per-
suaded the Clarendon Press at Oxford to cast a special font
of Minoan or—as he first described them—Mycenaean characters. These scripts became available to students all over
the world, but unfortunately not many of the three thou-
sand-odd tablets were published until 1934, and a further
batch in 1952.

One might ask why, since Cretan architecture and artifacts were so similar to what had been called Mycenaean, did Evans later make this distinction between Mycenaean and what he called Minoan? This was because, although the two forms of art were similar, there were subtle differences. The Mycenaeans fortified their citadels with strong walls. The Minoans, relying on their insular position, did not to the same extent, although there were defenses at Knossos.

But whereas the Cretan palaces were huge and rambling, with many rooms and interconnecting corridors, the Mycenaean buildings of the mainland were more compact, and were centered around a pillared hall or *megaron*. Again, the art betrayed differences. For instance, the scenes depicted on Mycenaean wall frescoes and on such weapons as were found at Mycenae are concerned mainly with hunting and fighting, as befitted a warrior people. Those depicted on the walls of Cretan palaces and on Cretan artifacts are usually of a more pacific nature. There is also an abundance of nautical scenes in Cretan art, usually lacking in that of the Mycenaeans.

Most important of all is the question of dating. Since Schliemann's time dating had become much more accurate. Evans was able to prove beyond any doubt that while the earliest Mycenaean cities developed not much earlier than 1700 B.C., those of Crete could be traced right back to the Middle Bronze Age (ca. 2100 B.C.), and even earlier settlements were found dating from the Neolithic period through the Early Bronze Age (ca. 4000–2000 B.C.). The priority of Cretan or Minoan dating, plus the obvious similarities between Cretan and Mycenean art, led Evans to believe that the so-called Mycenaean culture was a mere mainland offshoot of the island civilization, and that—as the legend of Theseus and the Minotaur suggests—the mainlanders may have been dominated by the islands.

125

This conclusion may not appear to have much relevance to the Linear A and Linear B scripts; but it has, because it led Evans and most archaeologists to believe that both scripts were Minoan, and therefore represented a dead language. Evans had in fact detected three forms of the script, an early hieroglyphic form found on the bead-seals, a more developed but still primitive picture writing (sometimes painted on vases), and the more advanced syllabic form which he had divided into the two categories "A" and "B." There seemed no doubt that the art of writing had grown up on the island, and Evans explained the difference between the "A" and "B" forms by suggesting that Linear B was a royal spelling system, used only at Knossos. In any case Ventris, when he began his work, had no reason to doubt Evans's belief that both languages were of Cretan origin.

However, before Ventris attended that historic lecture, a number of scholars, notably the late Professor Alan Wace, had begun to challenge Evans's theory that the so-called Mycenaean civilization was simply an offshoot of Cretan culture. Evans, like most scholars of his generation, believed that the first Greek-speaking people to enter Greece were the Dorians, who invaded the land in about 1100 B.C. Admittedly Schliemann and others had demonstrated that a rich civilization which they called Mycenaean had existed on the Greek mainland long before that time, but the Mycenaean invaders were presumed to have been non-Greek.

By the early thirties the technique of stratification on Greek and Cretan sites had advanced so far that archaeologists were able to date the various periods of both mainland and island culture by objects found in superimposed layers. This was made easier by the fact that sometimes Egyptian objects to which a fairly precise date could be given turned up, at sites like Knossos. In his excavations at Knossos Evans had distinguished four main periods. These were, from the bottom upwards:

Neolithic	ca. 4000–2700 B.C.	(when the inhabitants still used stone implements)
Early Minoan	2700–2000 B.C.	(Early Bronze Age)
Middle Minoan	2000–1600 B.C.	(Middle Bronze Age)
Late Minoan	1600–1200 B.C.	(Late Bronze Age)

These in turn are subdivided into Late Minoan I, II, and III; Middle Minoan I, II, and III, and so on, the terms usually being abbreviated to initials, EMI, EMII, EMIII. The building of the first Minoan palaces begins in the Middle Minoan period (2000 B.C.), and the destruction of the last Minoan palaces, either by earthquake, armed attack, or both, was in Late Minoan III (1400 B.C.). It is from this period that the Knossian clay tablets can be dated, since they were only found at this level and were baked in the fire which ravaged the palace.

Now let us consider the mainland sites such as Dimini in Thessaly, Asine, Eutresis, Eleusis, Korakou, and others which had been scientifically excavated by archaeologists of several nationalities. Here were found stratified layers which, from the type of pottery, tools, and weapons they contained, revealed four main periods, as in Crete. Although the dates do not exactly correspond with the Minoan dates (and are approximate anyway), scholars were able to define the Neolithic, Early Helladic, Middle and Late Helladic periods, each subdivided into three sections. The term Helladic applies to the mainland cultures, as Minoan is applied to the Cretan layers, and Cycladic to other island sites.

What is the significance of these layers of strata? Each

indicates a period of steady development extending over several centuries, during which the gradual evolution of pottery styles indicates that there has been no violent change. When a layer ends and an entirely new one begins as it did in the Greek mainland around 1900 B.C., there is evidence of sudden change. Pottery styles of an alien type replace their predecessors, tools and weapons are different. If one finds such evidence at a large number of separate sites around the same period, it is clear that there was an invasion by the people of another race or culture. From the researches of Wace and others, it became clear that this is what happened on the Greek mainland at this time. Wace wrote:

> By 1930 the archaeologists had, by studying the successive strata, come to accept generally the thesis that the Greeks must have first entered Greece at the beginning of the Middle Bronze Age, deducing this from the following facts . . .

Here he describes what he thinks happened before the Middle Bronze Age. The relevant passage is as follows:

> With the beginning of the Middle Bronze Age on the Mainland of Greece in the nineteenth century B.C. a new element appears. In the stratification of excavated sites such as Korakou, Eutresis and Lianokladi it is obvious that there is no transition or evolution from the early Bronze Age culture to that of the Middle Bronze Age. It is clear that a new factor at this time came into Greece; and since the material signs of its culture, pottery (which was made on the wheel), house plans, tombs, and in general all artifacts, differ markedly from those of the preceding Early Bronze Age, we assume that the differences mean a difference of race.

Wace and his colleagues believed that the invaders who entered Greece at the beginning of the Middle Bronze

Age were the ancestors of the Mycenaeans. Their course can be traced by a certain characteristic form of grey pottery called Grey Minyan which one finds on many mainland sites. Wace went on to suggest that it was the descendants of these people who built the strong-walled citadels at Mycenae, Tiryns, Thebes, Orchomenos, and elsewhere, beginning in about 1700 B.C., and reaching the peak of their power and influence between 1500 and 1250 B.C. Wace also postulated that these Mycenaeans, who belonged to the period known as Late Helladic III, came into contact with the Cretan culture and copied it, probably using Cretan workmen to fashion their works of art.

But there was no proof of this, and Evans and his followers stuck obstinately to the belief that the Minoans were the dominant race who had conquered and absorbed the mainland peoples, imposing their own culture upon them. The fact that Minoan Linear B writing tablets also began to turn up on mainland sites such as Mycenae and Pylos only reinforced Evans's conviction that the Cretans had been dominant, not only on their own island of Crete, but on the mainland as well. It was a strange fact that on the mainland only the writing system known as Linear B was found. Linear A was apparently confined to Knossos.

What young Ventris thought at this time I am not sure, but he appears to have followed Evans in believing that all these tablets, whether found in Crete or on the Greek mainland, represented the Minoan writing system and were therefore records of a dead language. He decided to concentrate his attention on Linear B rather than Linear A because the former was more widespread, appearing on mainland sites as well as at Knossos.

14 ✑ THE CHALLENGE OF LINEAR B

After leaving school, Michael Ventris decided to train as an architect. At first he lived alone in Highgate, London, and enrolled as a member of an architectural training school. There he met his future wife, Lois, with whom he fell in love; she too was an architectural trainee. Then the Second World War came. As soon as he was old enough, Michael enlisted in the Royal Air Force, and chose to be trained as a bomber navigator—"So much more interesting," he told me, "than being a driver," (i.e., a pilot). While waiting to be posted to his R.A.F. training school, he continued his architectural studies and married Lois, and before long their first child was on the way.

He lived in London during the terrible air raids of 1940 and managed, in intervals between fire-fighting, to produce a scholarly analysis of Linear B, a copy of which he sent to his former Classics teacher at Stowe. He also sent this article to a leading American archaeological journal, which published it in full. In later years Ventris regarded this article as rather adolescent, but the facts were accurately marshalled, and the closely reasoned arguments were supported by his brilliant drawings. It was a mature, scholarly analysis, in which Ventris suggested that the language had affinities with Etruscan (the pre-Roman language of Italy). In a note to his former teacher accompanying the offprint of this learned article, he said, "I did not tell them my age." He was then eighteen.

During his service with the Royal Air Force he took part in many bomber raids on Germany, seated at his navigator's table behind the pilot with his maps spread out before him. And not only his official R.A.F. maps; he once horrified his captain by navigating his way home with maps he had drawn himself. On numerous other occasions, when the bombing mission was completed and the bomber was groaning home through the flak, Ventris, after setting course, would take his Linear B documents out of his briefcase, spread them out on the table, and continue his research, a practice which speaks volumes for his calmness and ability to concentrate. The war over, he returned to his architectural studies, and qualified brilliantly as an architect, getting his diploma with honors in 1948. For a time he worked with the British Ministry of Education, designing new schools and undertaking private commissions.

Ventris accepted the general belief that both Linear A and Linear B were Cretan languages using the same script.

131

Yet they were different, as Dr. John Chadwick has pointed out:

> Though superficially alike, differences between the scripts are clear to a practiced eye; a very obvious difference is that the guidelines or rules that separate the lines of writing on Linear B tablets are absent in Linear A. A further difference concerns the numerical system. Linear A has a system of fractional signs, not yet fully worked out; Linear B has no signs of this type, but records fractional quantities in terms of smaller units . . . like dollars and cents. The difference between the systems of measurement was demonstrated with admirable clarity by Professor E. L. Bennett in 1950.

Emmett L. Bennett Jr. is an outstanding American scholar who contributed much to the final decipherment of Linear B, as did his colleague, the late Alice Kober of Brooklyn, a philologist who had studied the subject deeply for a number of years. The distinguished American archaeologist Professor Carl Blegen of the University of Cincinnati excavated, during the late thirties, a magnificent Mycenaean palace at Epano Englianos in the Peloponnese, which is almost certainly the Pylos described by Homer as the home of King Nestor. Here in 1939, just before the outbreak of the Second World War, Blegen came upon an archive room containing six hundred clay tablets, all inscribed in Linear B. It was the biggest haul of tablets ever made, and Blegen just had time to have them photographed before they were put in an Athens bank for safekeeping. But the photographs went to Emmett L. Bennett who studied, classified, and catalogued them.

It is important at this stage to understand that the method which Ventris adopted in his attempts to decipher

132

Linear B was not like that of Champollion with the hieroglyphs or Rawlinson with the cuneiform. In both those cases the scholars had a bilingual clue, or several bilingual clues. Therefore, since each had before him a known and an unknown language, his first efforts were directed to finding out if any of the phonetic values of the known writing could be identified in the unknown script. Later each went on to work out the grammar of the unknown language. This method had been tried by certain scholars in their attempts to decipher Linear B. In 1931 a British scholar named F. G. Gordon attempted to prove that the unknown language was related to the Basque tongue of Spain, on the grounds that Basque may have been a language spoken by Mediterranean peoples before the coming of languages based on Greek and Latin.

In his book *Through Basque to Minoan* Gordon attempted to assign the sound values of the Basque language to certain groups of Linear B signs, and he got some very peculiar results. For example, at Phaistos in southern Crete there had been discovered a strange baked clay disc inscribed spirally with an unknown form of writing, and some of the signs—not all—seemed similar to those hieroglyphic forms of the Minoan script. Even at the time of writing this book it has not been deciphered, but Gordon made a gallant attempt. His interpretation read as follows:

> . . . the lord walking on the wings of the breathless path, the star-smiter, the foaming gulf of waters, dogfish-smiter on the creeping flower, the dog emptying with its foot the water-pitchers, climbing the circling path, parching the wine-skin.

It is difficult to believe that this is a true translation or in-

133

*A clay disc with
pictographic characters
discovered at Phaestos.*

deed anything but fantasy. But it resulted from trying to apply phonetic values to a script before the grammatical structure was known.

Ventris's method of working on the script was quite different from that of most scholars engaged in the task. He argued that, lacking a bilingual clue, it was useless to attempt to assign phonetic values to Minoan signs until one had grasped the grammatical structure of the language. For instance, imagine that some future philologist, three thousand years hence, was trying to understand the grammar of the English language, even though he did not know what the signs meant or how the words were pronounced. Suppose he came upon the following group of signs often repeated:

G R O W

And a little further on he came upon the same group of signs, but with an additional one:

G R O W *N*

In another part of the script he might find the same first four signs repeated but with the addition of three more, thus:

G R O W *I N* G

Later he might notice another group of signs:

R O W

followed by other groups using the same first three characters but with different endings:

R O W *E D*
R O W *I N* G

He might guess that this was an inflected language, that the same word might have different endings or inflections to indicate, for example, the present or past tense, singular or plural. Again, he might ask about this unknown English language, does it have differences of gender? Does it distinguish between male and female—"his" or "hers," "he" or "she"?

Our investigator might find that *house* sometimes has an *s* at the end—*houses*—and might guess that this variant ending indicated the plural of the word. But how would he know, for instance, that the plural of *mouse* was not *mouses* but *mice*? If so, then why wasn't *hice* the plural of *house*? This illustrates just a few of the apparent anomalies in our own language which we take for granted. But they would add greatly to the problems of any later investigator. So it was with those who struggled for so many years with Linear B.

It was Alice Kober who first detected these variant endings, and she suggested, without attempting to assign sound values to the signs or indeed to relate them to any known language, that Minoan was an inflected language. Dr. Chadwick, the well-known English philologist who later cooperated with Ventris, says that had Alice Kober lived (she died at the age of forty-three) she might well have gone a long way towards achieving the decipherment, and that Ventris owed much to her.

Like Alice Kober's, Ventris's approach was essentially analytical and constructive. He was an architect, and his sense of form and construction enabled him to look at a building in a much more detailed way than most of us do. Whereas we see only the outer "skin" of the building, rows of windows and doors, perhaps pillars and porticoes, the trained architect can see through the outer skin and imagine what lies behind: the various floors, rooms, corridors, the steel girders of the inner structure, perhaps even the plumbing. He has to have a kind of X-ray eye. And having once absorbed these features he can hold them in his head, as if an image had been photographed on his brain.

Ventris's approach to the baffling Linear B signs was similar. Without understanding or attempting to understand their meaning, or the sounds they represented, he could, as it were, photograph whole groups of signs on his mental retina and seek for a coherent pattern in the whole. And, like Alice Kober, he thought that here and there he detected a consistent pattern; certain words occurred more often than others, just as our words *a* and *the* occur most often in this chapter. And then there were those variant endings or inflections.

It is typical of his openess and lack of guile that in 1950, having worked for fourteen years on the subject, he circulated the results of his research to twelve distinguished scholars whom he knew were similarly engaged, together with a questionnaire inviting them to express their opinions on certain matters which greatly concerned him. Had they any idea if the unknown language was related to a known tongue? In what way was it related to Linear A, if at all? Was it, in their opinion, an inflected language? It never seems to have occurred to him that some of the scholars, most of whom were personally unknown to him, might resent this approach and snub him. His attitude appears to have been, "Well, here we are all working on the same problem. This is what *I* think. Can we not work this thing out between us?"

The scholars were so disarmed by this fresh, frank approach, and by the brilliance of Ventris's own analysis of the problem, that only one of them failed to reply. He thought

137

he had broken the script already, and saw no reason to enter into correspondence. Alice Kober did not answer the questionnaire because, as she said later, it seemed quite pointless to discuss unproven theories. But like the others she was impressed by the preamble to the questionnaire, of which John Chadwick writes:

> The most interesting part of this document is the section by Ventris himself. In this he makes plain that the first step must be to establish the relationships between alternating signs, independently of the phoenetic values; all the rest, with the exception of Miss Kober, had concentrated on finding phonetic values, and the possibility of grouping the undeciphered signs had escaped them. The search for a pattern was the essential cryptographic procedure that made possible his success.

In that same year, 1950, Ventris seems almost to have given up. It was the fiftieth anniversary of Evans's discovery of the Knossian palace, and in a long article in his *Mid-Century Report* Ventris concluded with the words:

> I have good hopes that a sufficient number of people working on these lines will before long enable a satisfactory solution to be found. To them I offer my best wishes, being forced by pressure of other work to make this my last contribution to the problem.

All this time, of course, he had had to concentrate on his architectural work, and the decipherment of Linear B was secondary to this. And then in 1951 came one of those dramatic changes which prove that there is no certainty in life or in human endeavor. One of Ventris's main difficulties had been the lack of fresh material to work on. To the cryptographer and decipherer one of the main dangers is what Ventris called "circular reasoning." Let us revert once again to our future philologist trying to decipher the unknown English language without a bilingual clue. Imagine that he had only twenty or thirty pages of the unknown writing on which to work. He might be able to assign provisional values to the signs. "This is my theory," he might say, "and within the limits of the available material it appears to work." Only if he found an abundance of new pages, which he had not seen before, could he test his theory and see if it really stood up.

This is what happened in 1951, when Emmett L. Bennett published the six hundred tablets which Blegen had found at Pylos in 1939, carefully classified and catalogued. And in the following year Blegen, renewing his excavations at Pylos, found the other end of the archive room and unearthed four hundred more tablets, all in Linear B. One thousand newly published tablets were now available for study! Bennett and Ventris, both young men, living on opposite sides of the Atlantic, began an eager correspondence. The new discoveries gave Ventris fresh heart. He was not giving up the struggle.

15 ～ TRIUMPH
AND
TRAGEDY

During the years 1951 to 1954 Ventris, at his own expense, circulated the results of his research to all interested scholars at regular intervals. In all, these notes totalled 176 pages. The lack of any selfish, competitive motive is quite remarkable, and represents the best tradition of international scholarship (which is not invariably observed). His method of attack on the Linear B script remained the same—to establish first the grammatical pattern of the unknown language, the rules it observed, and the way it was put together, before attempting to assign sound values to its characters, or to relate it to any known language or group of languages. This is a very difficult concept, and few of his fellow researchers were able or willing to follow it, since it involved years of laborious research; it was much more tempting to attempt to substitute the phonetic values of a known language experimentally, and see if they could be made to fit the Linear B pattern. Several such attempts were made and all failed. In fact Ventris's method was more akin to that of an engineer or mathematician than that of a linguist.

Sooner or later he knew he would have to attempt to assign phonetic values to the signs, or the script would never be read. In the meantime, during the fifteen months following Bennett's publication of the Pylos tablets, he studied and absorbed the new material whenever he could spare time from his architectural work, corresponding eagerly with other scholars, and circulating his notes to them. Often he would work far into the night on this research, since his days were more than fully occupied with the duties of his profession. Of this period of his work, Ventris wrote:

> Once the values of a syllabary are known, its signs can be most conveniently set out in the form of a chequerboard "grid" on which the vertical columns each contain a single vowel, and the horizontal lines a single consonant. A vital part of the analysis consisted of arranging the signs as far as possible in the correct pattern before any phonetic values were tried out; this was made possible by clear evidence that certain groups of signs shared the same vowel, (e.g. *no ro to*) others the same consonant (e.g. *wa wi wo*).

Miss Kober had noticed that certain groups of signs occurred repeatedly in the Knossian tablets, but she pointed out that, although similar, they did not always take the same form; there were variant endings. Ventris knew that among the principal cities of Minoan Crete were the following:

141

Amnissos
Knossos
Tylissos
Phaestos
Lyktos

In a paper published in *Antiquity* in December 1953, Ventris wrote:

. . . it is characteristic of most languages, when syllabically written, that the signs for the plain vowels A.E.I.O.U. are exceptionally common in the initial position; and the first "triplet" (Ventris's name for Miss Kober's selected group of words) suggested the value "A" to Kober and Kristopoulos (another linguist). The decisive step was to identify the first words with Amnissos, and to substitute values which would turn the others into Knossos, Tylissos, Phaestos and Lyktos:

A-mi-ni-so	*Ko-no-so*	*Tu-ri-so*	*Pa-i-to*	*Ru-ki-to*
A-mi-ni-so-jo	*Ko-no-si-jo*	*Tu-ri-si-jo*	*Pa-to-jo*	*Ru-ki-ti-jo*
A-mi-ni-si-ja	*Ko-no-si-ja*	*Tu-ri-si-ja*	*Pa-i-ti-ja*	*Ru-ki-ti-ja*

Since about fifty signs had already been assigned to their places on the "grid" the substitution of these five words automatically fixed most of them as well, by a kind of chain reaction. If these names were an illusion, then the resulting system of values must inevitably be a completely dislocated jumble, with which no further sense could be extracted by any sort of jugglery.

Now these five Cretan proper names do not sound exciting in themselves; but in fact, as Ventris wrote, they set off a kind of chain reaction because, as he goes on to say, "they fell into line, not merely with the known Greek system of declensions, but specifically with its most archaic forms as deduced from Homeric and other dialects."

Ventris was astonished. He had not started, as some decipherers had, with the idea that the unknown language was Greek; on the contrary, he tended to favor Etruscan origins. Not being an archaeologist, he was not influenced by the belief of Wace and others, passionately urged, that the Mycenaeans were of Greek origin. His method had been to analyze the structure of the language and only then to determine by experiment whether it could be related to any surviving language or group of languages. But the more he experimented, the more he was forced to accept the fact that, to all appearances, the language of the unknown script was Greek. When he tried to apply the same system of decipherment to Linear A it did not work. As Linear B had been found at several places on the mainland, while Linear A was only known at Knossos, the suspicion that Linear B was a very early form of Greek grew even stronger.

Ventris had learned classical Greek at school, where he had been an average student, but the Linear B script differed from classical Greek in ways which might well be explained by its great age. Classical Greek only began in the eighth century B.C. By comparison Minoan (or Mycenaean) Greek was as remote as Anglo-Saxon is from modern English. As Dr. John Chadwick points out in his *Decipherment of Linear B*, classical Greek is in the main the speech of Athens—the dialect of Attica—but there were other dialects. For instance, there was the Ionic dialect in which Homer wrote. The word for "boy" in Ionic is *kouros;* in the dialect of Attica it is *koros*. Probably the original form was *korwos,* of which the feminine form *korwa* survived in the Arcadian dialect of Greece.

It is at this point, in June 1952, that John Chadwick entered the scene. He is a gentle, mild-mannered Cambridge scholar, a specialist in ancient Greek dialects, who for some years had pondered over the problem of the Cretan scripts. One night he happened to be listening to a broadcast of the British Broadcasting Corporation. Michael Ventris was talking and he said something which made Chadwick sit up in his chair:

> During the last few weeks I have come to the conclusion that the Knossos and Pylos tablets must, after all, be written in Greek—a difficult and archaic Greek, seeing that it is five hundred years older than Homer and written in a rather abbreviated form, but Greek nevertheless.

> Once I made this assumption, most of the peculiarities of the language and spelling which had puzzled me seemed to find a logical explanation; and although many of the tablets remain as incomprehensible as before many others are· suddenly beginning to make sense.

And Ventris cited a number of words which he had deciphered from the tablets as Greek, e.g. *poimen* ("shepherd") and *kerameus* ("potter"). Then there was the strange word *khrusoworgos* ("goldsmith"). It was this last word which attracted Chadwick's particular attention. He admits that he did not regard Ventris's chances highly, and though he (Chadwick) thought he had a pretty good idea of what Mycenaean Greek would look like, he doubted if Ventris had. For Ventris was not a Greek philologist, as Chadwick was, with a specialized knowledge of Greek dialect forms. But, as the latter wrote, "the word *khrusoworgos* . . . was encouraging; the sound *w* did not exist in most forms of Greek of the classical period, but should certainly appear in an archaic dialect since its loss, as in Homer, was known to be recent."

Chadwick was thirty-two at the time; Ventris was thirty. The Cambridge scholar got in touch with Ventris, and so began a collaboration which was both friendly and fruitful. The sceptical scholar was impressed by the charm, modesty, and intellectual power of the brilliant amateur. Ventris, on his side, was grateful for the help which Chadwick, with his profound knowledge of ancient Greek, could provide. He wrote in a letter to Chadwick:

> At the moment I feel rather in need of moral support . . .
> I'm conscious that there's a *lot* which so far can't be satis-
> factorily explained.

Chadwick also quotes another letter received from Ventris at about this time.

> I've been feeling the need of a "mere philologist" (Chad-
> wick's description of himself to Ventris) to keep me on the
> right lines. . . . I'm glad that your view of some of the
> phonetic values coincides with my own, though I suppose
> a court of law might suppose I'd pre-cooked the material
> in such a way that coincidence wasn't conclusive.

Chadwick reassured him on this point. If, he pointed out, both had suggested the same phonetic values independently (as they had), then only two conclusions were possible: either they were right and the decipherment was proved, or else Ventris had deliberately planted the evidence for others to find. "One had only to make Ventris's acquaintance," says Chadwick, "to realise that the latter alternative was out of the question."

For a time it seemed almost as if Chadwick and Ventris had changed places. Chadwick became more and more convinced that Ventris's decipherment was right; Ventris began to be plagued by doubts about his own work. Why, he asked, if this was Greek, did it lack the definite article, the word "the" which was present in the classical Greek he had learned at school? Again Chadwick reassured him. Philologists, he explained, had already anticipated that it would be

145

absent in the early stages of the language. Then Chadwick detected what he believed to be the name of a well-known Greek goddess on one of the tablets. Ventris objected:

> I've a rooted objection to finding gods' names on the tablets . . . but *Athana potnia* (the lady Athena) certainly looks too good to be true.

So the arguments went on, but Chadwick comments that "in an amazingly short time Ventris had mastered the details of Greek philology for himself." He drew up his *Experimental Vocabulary* with 533 entries, most of which have since been definitely established, despite the scrutiny to which his work was rightly subjected once it had been published. But although articles appeared in journals, Chadwick and his colleague worked for two years on the preparation of their big definitive book, a work of formidable learning covering nearly five hundred pages, entitled *Documents in Mycenaean Greek*. It was not published until 1956, and made a tremendous impression among scholars throughout the world. The vast majority have come to accept its conclusions, though a few remain unconvinced.

There were at least two moments in Ventris's tragically short life when he was roused from his customary calm. One was when the hidden language gradually revealed itself as Greek when, after some fourteen years' labor, and all his work on the "grid," he at last tried experimental substitution of actual sounds. The second occurred in 1952 when Professor Blegen, having returned to Pylos, found a hoard of new tablets and, using Ventris's system, experimented with their decipherment. He found one with pictograms clearly depicting pots of various kinds. Of this tablet Blegen wrote to Ventris:

146

Since my return to Greece I have spent much of my time working on the tablets . . . getting them properly ready to be photographed. I have tried your experimental syllabary on them. Enclosed for your information is a copy of tablet P641, which you may find interesting. It evidently deals with pots, some on three legs, some with four handles, some with three, others without handles. The first word, by your system, seems to be *ti-ro-po-de* (tripod) and it recurs twice as *ti-ri-po* (singular?). The four-handled pot is preceded by *que-to-ro-we*, the three-handled by *ti-ro-o-we* or *ti-ri-jo-we*, the handleless pot by *an-no-we*. All this seems to be too good to be true. Is coincidence excluded?

The famous Linear B tablet from Pylos.

This tablet has been called the Rosetta Stone of Linear B. Here was entirely fresh material, not previously seen by Ventris, which proved to read as archaic Greek, just like the other tablets which Ventris had conjecturally deciphered. Even the reader with no Greek can appreciate this, for the syllables *on, tri,* and *que* can be equated with our English *one* and *three,* and the French *quatre.* On receiving this precious information Ventris immediately telephoned Chadwick at Cambridge, and his friend said afterwards: "Michael was in a great state of excitement—he rarely showed emotion but this for him was a dramatic moment."

Another wonderful moment for Ventris was when he was invited to lecture at Uppsala in Sweden, where he received an honorary Doctorate of Philosophy from the university. Scholars were present from many parts of the world, some of whom had labored for years—as many years as Ventris—to wrest the secret from the Linear B tablets. When the now famous "Tripod Tablet" was flashed on the screen during the course of the lecture, the whole audience got up and cheered him. This demonstrative behavior is rare among scholars. When John Chadwick asked Michael how the lecture had been received he merely replied, "Oh, quite well." Among the honors he received at this time was an O.B.E. (Order of the British Empire) "for services to Mycenaean palaeography." Other distinctions would no doubt have followed had he lived.

Then came a day I shall never forget. Not long after the publication of *Documents in Mycenaean Greek* I walked into the headquarters of the Society for the Promotion of Hellenic Studies, London, and was greeted by a visibly shaken assistant with the words, "Mr. Cottrell, have you heard? Mr. Ventris was killed in a road accident yesterday." It was true. Returning to London late at night after giving a lecture, tired after a long journey, Ventris must have dozed over the wheel of his car. It hit the back of a truck and he was killed instantly. He was thirty-four.

Since that time *Documents in Mycenaean Greek* has stood up well to the critical scrutiny of scholars. Some of Ventris's decipherments have had to be amended or discarded in the light of more recent research, but this is what he would have expected and indeed wished. As he hoped, other linguists have taken up the torch where he had to leave it. Scholars continue to argue in learned papers and at international seminars about the exact interpretation of this or that word. But the bulk of his work remains unshaken. He made the breakthrough and others have followed him eagerly through the breach. Had he lived he might have gone on to tackle Linear A, and there were rumors just before his death that he had interested himself in the still undeciphered language written by the prehistoric inhabitants of the Indus Valley civilization in India.

Whatever he might or might not have achieved, he made a contribution to Greek scholarship which has few equals. In the words of Professor Dumézil of France in an historic obituary address: *"Devant les siècles son oeuvre est faite."* Which freely translated means, "His work stands secure before future centuries."

16 ～ WAS IT
WORTH IT?

"Horse-vehicle, painted red, with bodywork fitted, supplied with reins; the rail(?) of wild fig-wood with jointing of horn; and the *pte-no* is missing; 1 CHARIOT."

That is a translation of a typical Linear B tablet from the armory at Knossos.

There are over four thousand tablets. Nearly all are inventories like the above, or they record allocations of land, tax or tribute paid to this or that individual (sometimes a god or goddess), or they give brief details of military or naval movements, or they list numbers of slaves, men and women, numbers of "corselets," "swords," "horses." All have this in common: they are records of mundane occupations and activities, nothing more. And yet this, according to the archaeologists and historians, was the heroic age of Greece, the period of which Homer wrote. Where then is the heroic literature which one might suppose to have existed? If it did exist, it has yet to be found.

Compared with the wealth of rich literary material released by the decipherment of Egyptian hieroglyphs and Babylonian cuneiform, the content of the Linear B tablets is trivial. And this fact, though it was forecast by Evans who early recognized that the tablets were palace store lists, may seem at first disappointing. It is almost as if, having been told that a manuscript of one of Shakespeare's plays had been found, it turned out to be his laundry list. Yet the matter is not quite as simple as that. A great deal has been and is being learned from the tablets about the Mycenaean world, far more than would appear at first glance.

For instance, it is fascinating to find among the proper names given in the tablets many which are familiar in Homer: such names as Hector, Achilles, Zeus, Hera, Hermes, Athena, and Artemis, besides many others. Very often, however, the bearers of these illustrious names are employed in quite modest occupations. This, however, is hardly surprising; one does not automatically think of King George III or George Washington when one hears the name "George." And no doubt many ordinary men and women were named after heroes and heroines, just as today some people give their children the names of prominent personalities.

That each state was ruled by a monarch, as described by Homer, is confirmed by the frequent occurrence of the word *wanax* (king). It is disappointing that so far the name Nestor has not yet turned up at Pylos, though we have the name of one Pylian monarch, Ekhelawon, the first contemporarily attested Mycenaean king. Next to the king in rank appears to have been the *lawagetas*, who had the duty of leading the army in war—a military commander. Then there was an official called the *e-qu-ta*, which in classical Greek means no more than "companion" or "follower." However, the well-known philologist Professor Leonard Palmer has put forward strong reasons for thinking that in its Linear B context this word means "Companion of the King," like the Latin *comes* or the English "Count." Lower down the scale were numerous other officials in descending scale of rank, until one comes to the ordinary people.

The variety of trades and occupations is astonishing; the tablets tell us of shepherds, goatherds, woodcutters, huntsmen, masons, carpenters, ship-builders, bronzesmiths, bow-makers, chair(?)-makers, and weavers; also flax-workers, fullers, garment-makers, unguent-boilers, goldsmiths, bread-makers, and among the more humble occupations, stokers, ox-drivers, serving-women, and bath-attendants (who were also women).

These by no means exhaust the list; there are many more trades and occupations, revealing how complex and civilized Mycenaean society was, with so much specialization. In fact, one of the puzzling facts is that it gives an impression of a society far more bureaucratic and highly organized than that depicted by Homer in the *Iliad* and the *Odyssey*. Yet this need not surprise us. Homer was writing some four centuries after the events he described, and those events were mainly concerned with war, travel, and adventure. He wanted to give his readers or listeners a good tale, full of action and suspense. Why should he have concerned himself with carpenters, unguent-boilers, stokers, and bath-attendants, even if he had known about them? Probably he did not know about them, or about Mycenaean bureaucracy with its record-keepers and tax-collectors, since he himself, and his audience, lived in a much simpler society. The epics themselves, according to general belief, had been passed on to him by generations of bards or poets who kept them alive during a period when the art of writing had vanished, only to be revived when the Greeks of classical times learned the alphabet through the Phoenicians.

And yet one wonders if in fact there was a time when not only mundane household records, but also stories, poetry, and history were recorded in the Mycenaean writing system. It has been pointed out that the Linear B script seems to have been designed to be written with a pen on some smooth material such as skin or papyrus, and not incised on clay. The shape of some of the tablets, roughly that of a palm leaf, reminds one of Pliny's statement that the Cretans had originally written on palm leaves. Again, as Chadwick points out,

> Many of the Minoan clay sealings have the impression of thin strings, perhaps securing papyrus, on one face; and clay sealings from the 1948 excavations at Sklavokampos near Knossos show impressions from identical seal-stones as sealings found at Agia Triada, Gournia and Zakro (all in Crete) proving an exchange of correspondence between these sites.

The Minoans and Mycenaeans were in contact with Egypt and western Asia. Imported Cretan and Mycenaean manufactures have been found in both areas, and in certain Egyptian tombs of ca. 1500 B.C. there are paintings clearly depicting Minoan officials carrying the typical products of their country to the Pharaoh. The style of dress of these men is exactly matched by the wall frescoes found by Evans in the palace of Knossos. This proves that the Minoans (and the Mycenaeans, as we know from other sources) knew Egypt and the Levant; indeed, as a seafaring people, this is

153

an obvious conclusion. One would have thought that the learned scribes of Minoan Crete and Mycenaean Greece would have corresponded with the Egyptians, just as we know from Tell el Amarna that the Egyptian scribes could write or read Babylonian cuneiform, and kept records of correspondence.

So there is just a faint chance that some day an Egyptologist may stumble upon a papyrus scroll written in Linear B preserved by the dry climate of Egypt. The chance of writing on such perishable material, whether skin, palm leaves, or papyrus, having survived in the damper climate of Crete and Greece is extremely remote. Why, it may be asked, should the Linear B records have been incised on wet clay and left to dry in the sun? The most likely answer, given by Chadwick (though I think I detect here the practical mind of Michael Ventris), is mice. These store-room records, which in the case of the Pylian palace were found in a small archive chamber just within the main entrance, were never intended to be kept for more than a year, after which they were pulped and fresh tablets made. What could be more natural then, than to keep them on clay tablets which were invulnerable to mice and termites?

It was only the fire that destroyed the palace which preserved them. At Pylos they were found scattered on the floor of the chamber, baked hard by the heat. Originally they had been stored on shelves in boxes of gypsum, wood or wicker-work, the impressions of which remained on the clay in some cases. They were office files, just like those in a modern commercial office. At Knossos they were found in other places besides the administrative quarter, but this, as Evans suggested, must have been due to some tablets' having been stored in upper rooms which had collapsed. Again, only the fire which destroyed the palace when the invaders sacked it preserved the tablets for posterity.

Some authorities incline to the view that the art of writing was never lost, even when the Dorians invaded Greece and destroyed the old Mycenaean civilization. It is possible, these authorities think, that the literature of the Mycenaean period was preserved in a few places down to Homer's time, the Greeks being too intelligent a people to let such a useful instrument as writing be forgotten. There may be something in this, but if so, why was the Linear B system not preserved? Why did the Greeks of the classical period write in a new alphabetic script based on that of the Phoenicians, unless it was because the alphabetic script is so much more convenient to use than the syllabary of the Minoans and the Mycenaeans, and the latter was therefore abandoned? It is an interesting fact that in the remote island of Cyprus a syllabary continued to be used even in classical times, and there are remote resemblances in it to Linear B.

There is, however, another point of view, which I tend to favor. It is that in Minoan and Mycenaean times writing was not highly regarded, and was considered an occupation fit only for storekeepers. Literature may have been transmitted by word of mouth, the bards preserving for generations the myths, folk tales and epic poems with which they delighted their courtly audiences. This is a difficult concept for us to accept, so conditioned are we to writing, but this custom is common in unsophisticated societies. Even in our own day we take it for granted that an experienced actor can commit the whole of *Hamlet* to memory. If this theory is true, it would explain why certain aspects of Mycenaean civilization which are evident from the tablets were forgotten or ignored in the poems of Homer. Each generation

155

would expect the story told by the bard to be kept up to date. For example, the Greeks of classical times cremated their royal and princely dead; therefore in the *Iliad* the body of Achilles' friend Patroclus was burned, whereas we know that the Mycenaeans buried their great men.

On the other hand, although Homer's heroes march into battle behind round shields, which were in use at his period, they also use bronze weapons, which had gone out of use, and fought from chariots, which again we know was the usual form in Mycenaean times but not at the time of Homer. Enough of the Mycenaean past was preserved to give the poems authenticity and realism, while at the same time unimportant anachronisms crept in. In my view, if the poems had been transmitted through four centuries in written form, these discrepancies would not have occurred. All this suggests that whereas writing was used by clerks and record-keepers, what we call literature was passed on orally.

Another strange fact inclines me to this point of view. In ancient Egypt, palaces, temples, and tombs were inscribed, often very lavishly; some were almost covered with written inscriptions. The same is true of the ancient monuments of Babylonia and Assyria. Yet the Minoans and Mycenaeans, who were in contact with these other civilizations —certainly with that of Egypt—never did likewise. You will look in vain for any sign of writing on a Minoan or Mycenaean palace, nor are there inscribed stones outside or inside their tombs. The painted frescoes like those on the walls of the Knossian palace, the bull-leaping fresco, the procession of young men, the court ladies engaged in animated conversation—none of these has a single line of writing. Could there perhaps have been some religious taboo which forbade the use of writing on such buildings?

Then we come to this question: Why were the Linear B

Beautiful paintings, such as this, were found on the walls of the palace of Knossos.

tablets written in Greek if, as Evans passionately believed, both Linear A and Linear B were Cretan writing systems, and if the Mycenaeans of the mainland were a cultural off-shoot of the island Minoans? It became clear, as a result of Ventris's achievement, that Wace's theory—that the Mycenaeans were a Greek-speaking people—is valid. He had sought to prove it by archaeological evidence alone. Then the philologists came to give him support. For it must be significant that although Linear A is only found at Knossos, Linear B is found in Crete and at several important mainland sites. The Mycenaeans represented a separate culture, and their ancestors were the first Greek-speaking people to enter Greece at the beginning of the Middle Bronze Age (Middle Helladic I, about 2000 B.C.).

The significance of this is enormous, for it means that the Greek civilization and language go back not a mere twenty-six hundred years but nearer four thousand, and are without doubt the oldest in Europe and among the oldest in the world. Cretan civilization began even earlier, and the similarity between Cretan and Mycenaean art, architecture, and customs can be explained by the assumption that the incoming Greeks, Homer's "Achaeans," came into contact with the older culture and copied it, although the Mycenaeans appear to have been a hardier, more warlike race who eventually conquered Crete.

As for Linear A, it remains as a challenge to a new generation of decipherers because, to date, no one has succeeded in interpreting it. Possibly it will never be deciphered, as it may represent the lost language of ancient Crete which passed out of use after the Mycenaeans occupied the island. Even this theory, however, presents problems and difficulties. In the first place, according to Evans's dating, the palaces of Knossos, Phaestos, Mallia and else-

where were all destroyed in around 1400 B.C., and he firmly
dated the Knossian tablets to this period. But if Greek was
in use in 1400 B.C., then the Greeks must have been in Crete
before that date.

There is, however, an intellectual challenge here. It
would be so much more convenient if the Knossos tablets
could be dated to about 1200 B.C., as the Pylos tablets are.
In fact, within recent years Professor Palmer, an English
philologist from Oxford and a redoubtable authority on the
Greek language, has argued forcibly that Evans must have
been wrong in his dating, and that the civilization of Crete
lasted down to 1200 B.C. or even later. Evans said, based on
the archaeological evidence, that after the major catastrophe which overtook Knossos and other sites in 1400 B.C. the
palaces were occupied only by "squatters" who lived in the
ruins, dividing up the great rooms, just like poor families
today taking over abandoned buildings. The tablets found
scattered in many parts of the ruins were, without doubt, all
baked (and so preserved) in the fire which ravaged the
building, whenever that catastrophe took place; they were
not written after it.

Palmer argues that the destruction of the palaces took
place nearer 1200 B.C. than 1400, but here he has been op-
posed by the archaeologist Dr. John Boardman, who, after
examining the records of Evans's "dig" and the site itself, remains convinced that Evans's dating was substantially correct. He bases this belief on expert knowledge, and Professor Palmer, who is not an archaeologist, has not, in the
opinion of most scholars, succeeded in confuting him. What
adds weight to Boardman's opinion is the fact that originally Professor Palmer enlisted Boardman's professional skill
in elucidating this mystery, and at first Boardman was quite
prepared to accept Palmer's theory provided it could be

proved on archaeological grounds. But the more deeply he went into the subject, the more certain he became that Evans's dating was substantially correct, and so far no one has been able to prove that the Knossos tablets are of the same date as the Pylos tablets, which can definitely be dated to ca. 1200 B.C., when this Mycenaean palace was destroyed by invaders, presumably the first wave of "Dorian" Greeks.

Another interesting theory, put forward by Professor Spyridon Marinatos, director of the Antiquities Department of the Greek government, is that the destruction of Minoan civilization was connected with the volcanic eruption of the island of Thera, about seventy miles away, in about 1500 B.C. The remains of this island, now called Santorin, surround a deep undersea crater of vast depth. It has been calculated that the volcanic force required to blow up this island and form the crater must have been several times greater than that which destroyed the island of Krakatoa in the eighteen-eighties. That catastrophe caused immense tidal waves which flung heavy railway locomotives off their tracks, wrecked the coastal cities of Java and Sumatra, and tossed a substantial steamer some distance inland. The volcanic dust erupted by Krakatoa circled the earth for several years.

One can easily imagine the effect of such an eruption in about 1550–1500 B.C., the estimated dates. The tidal waves would have been sufficient to destroy the ports and the Minoan fleet, on which the islanders relied for their defense. Earth tremors would have caused great damage to the palaces, and probably fires. The violent earthquakes, the pall of volcanic dust blotting out the sky, the deep underground rumbling "like the muffled roar of an angry bull," such as Evans noted in an earthquake which struck the island in the twenties, would have combined to produce a moral effect on the Cretans beyond anything we—with our glib explanations of "natural forces"—would have experienced. To them it must have seemed that the god Poseidon, of whom Homer wrote "In Bulls doth the Earth-Shaker delight," had determined to annihilate them.

It therefore seems probable that, demoralized by the catastrophe, stripped of their defenses, the Minoans might well have succumbed to a determined attack by the Mycenaeans. But if the eruption took place even as late as 1500 B.C., this would mean that the Mycenaean sacking of Knossos took place earlier than 1400, for in a century the Minoan Empire would have had the opportunity to recover. Or possibly there may have been another earthquake around that date. Here again we enter the realm of speculation. And it still does not explain what the Greeks were doing in Crete as early as 1400, since, according to Evans and Boardman, that was the approximate date of the Knossos Linear B tablets.

17 ❧ SUMMING UP

In the introduction to this book we said that we should concentrate on the decipherment of the three oldest known languages and on the three oldest known civilizations, and in each case try to show how the decipherment was achieved, what kind of civilization was revealed by the decipherment, and why civilization, and the art of writing, grew up in that particular region. For a long time it was thought that there had been no civilization in Europe comparable in age and splendor with those of Babylonia and ancient Egypt. Evans's discoveries in Crete, and those of his successors, have proved conclusively that this opinion was wrong. The Cretan civilization may not have been quite as old as that of ancient Egypt, but substantial palaces were being built there as early as 2000 B.C., and occupation levels go back much further than that, perhaps to 4000 B.C.

Mycenaean culture, though not so old, reached its apogee during the period 1500–1200 B.C., roughly contemporary with the Eighteenth and Nineteenth Dynasties of ancient Egypt. It is thought that the Mycenaean gold found by Schliemann in the shaft-graves at Mycenae may have been from Egypt, acquired by trade with that country. Both Cretan and Mycenaean objects have been found in Egypt, and Egyptian objects in Crete. The Cretans must also have had trade contacts with Babylonia, since Babylonian cylinder seals have been found in Cretan deposits. Cretan and Mycenaean artifacts have also been found at such places as Ugarit, on the coast of Syria, where writing was known, and there is evidence that the Mycenaeans or Achaeans were in contact with the kings of the Hittite empire in Asia Minor, which was also literate.

This brings us to the question: What was the origin of the Cretan writing system, subsequently adopted by the Mycenaean Greeks? Of course both Linear A and Linear B are relatively late cursive developments of a much earlier writing system, which was pictographic and hieroglyphic. There is little to connect such Cretan hieroglyphs as have been found with the hieroglyphs of ancient Egypt, though Chadwick and Ventris say cautiously that "the Cretan hieroglyphs probably show some influence from Egyptian models." The idea of writing may have been brought to the island by early immigrants, some of whom, according to Evans, probably came from Egypt and Libya while others arrived from Syria. In Egypt, as we have shown, primitive hieroglyphs were being used as far back as the reign of Narmer or Hor-Aha (ca. 3200 B.C.), and there have even been suggestions that some of the earliest settlers in Crete may have been refugees from the Delta or northern region of Egypt, driven out when Hor-Aha conquered the land of Lower Egypt around about 3200 B.C.

On the other hand, the earliest known examples of Cretan hieroglyphs occur at the beginning of Middle Minoan, around 2000 B.C., when writing had existed in Egypt for over a thousand years. Even the surviving records are very scanty, consisting mainly of seal impressions on clay. Later, one finds seal-stones engraved with one to six signs in a more advanced hieroglyphic script, and "a more cursive form of this script began to be incised on clay, mostly in the form of circular labels or rectangular bars, both of these being pierced for attachment by strings." These appear to date from Middle Minoan II (ca. 1850–1700 B.C.).

The first examples of Linear A occur during Middle Minoan IIIb (ca. 1660–1580 B.C.).

As for why civilization developed so early in Crete, and not elsewhere in the Greek archipelago, the following facts should be borne in mind. First, Crete is roughly equidistant from Egypt and western Asia, where civilization had begun as early as 3000 B.C. Second, as Homer truly said, it was "a rich and lovely land" abounding in natural resources, agricultural land, timber, and stone for building, and it was big enough to support a large, independent population. Third, it was sufficiently remote to be protected from enemies by a people who had built a powerful fleet, since no invasion was possible except by sea. Yet most of these facts apply equally to Cyprus, another large island even nearer Asia, where there is as yet no evidence of the early development of civilization comparable to that of Crete. Here is another mystery.

Certainly there must have been immigrants from the coast of what is now Syria, Israel, and Lebanon, and these people spoke a Semitic tongue. Professor Cyrus Gordon, in his book *Forgotten Scripts*, makes this positive statement:

> Minoan Linear A is identified as Northwest Semitic, and though its texts are limited in number and scope, the very fact of its identification will have a major effect on our understanding of ancient history. There is hope that literary texts in Minoan will be found. A poetic tablet from Enkomi, Cyprus, of the Late Bronze Age shows that the Aegaean script was used for literary texts.

Professor Gordon also cites a fascinating story from one Lucius Septimus, who lived in the fourth century A.D. This writer avers that in the time of Nero a literary text was found at Knossos. It was written in a form of Phoenician, and Nero, who fancied himself a *littérateur,* called in experts in the Semitic writing system to translate it. According to the story the text turned out to be an account of Dictys of Crete, a hero of the Trojan War. Lucius Septimus gave a

Latin rendition of the Greek translation, which was condemned as spurious. Professor Gordon comments:

> After the condemnation, however, papyri of an earlier date were found in Egypt giving an older Greek version of *Dictys Cretensis*. It will be no source of surprise if, as has happened so many times, the ancient sources are correct and the Greek was translated from the Semitic original that had been found at Knossos and transmitted to Nero.

If there is one common factor in all the stories of decipherment, setting aside for a moment the immense and laborious technical difficulties of the work, it is that of surprise, that sudden, unexpected revelation, like a shaft of sunlight penetrating thick clouds, which brings a glow to the heart of the investigator. Such was the moment when Grotefend recognized the names of ancient Persian kings in the Persepolitan syllabary; the moment when Champollion was able to read the names of well-known Pharaohs like Rameses and Tuthmosis in the Egyptian hieroglyphs; the moment when Michael Ventris, after seventeen years of laborious striving with the baffling Minoan signary, suddenly saw Cretan names appearing in the script and obeying the laws of the Greek language, *A-mi-ni-so, A-mi-ni-so-jo, A-mi-ni-si-ja,* or when he received Blegen's Tripod Tablet and saw beside a pictogram of a three-legged pot Linear B signs which read *Ti-ri-po-de*. But such moments are rare for the decipherer.

Another common factor is the surprising youth of many of the great decipherers. Thomas Young had mastered twelve languages by the time he was twenty. Champollion read his first scientific paper to the Grenoble Academy when he was fourteen, became professor of history at eighteen and published his great work *Précis du Système Hiéroglyphique* when he was thirty-four. And Ventris, as we have seen, began work on Linear B when he was fourteen and published his decipherment when he was thirty-four, the year of his tragic death.

It would seem, therefore, that the most promising years of the would-be decipherer's life are his youthful ones, before his mental arteries harden, and while his mind is still flexible and agile enough to accept new ideas or discard old theories. There is still plenty of material to work on. There is the Etruscan language; there are the Hittite hieroglyphs; there is the language written by the people of the Indus Valley civilization; and there is, of course, Linear A, which —though identified as a language having affinities with the northwest Semitic group, such as Ugaritic—has not yet been deciphered. I therefore end this book by wishing the best of luck to all who may in the future attempt the toilsome, hazardous, but absorbing task of reading the past.

❧ GUIDE TO
FURTHER READING

✌ GUIDE TO FURTHER READING

The following brief selection of books has been made mainly with the general reader in mind. However, even some of the more technical books, such as *Documents in Mycenaean Greek*, contain chapters which are readily assimilable by non-specialists, and such books have been marked with an asterisk. Most of the works listed deal with several ancient languages, including some not mentioned in this book. Others are concerned with some specific area of research, such as Egypt, Babylonia, or Greece, and these are separately classified.

GENERAL

Ceram, C. W. *Gods, Graves and Scholars*. New York: Knopf, 1967.

Childe, V. G. *The Dawn of European Civilization*. New York: Knopf, 1958.

Cleator, P. E. *Lost Languages*. London: Robert Hale Ltd., 1959.

°Diringer, D. *The Alphabet*. London: Hutchinson, 1952.

———. *Writing*. London: Thames and Hudson, 1962.

Doblhofer, E. *Voices in Stone.* New York: Viking, 1961.

°Gelb, I. J. *A Study of Writing.* Chicago: University of Chicago Press, 1942.

Gordon, C. H. *Forgotten Scripts.* London: Thames and Hudson, 1968.

Griffith, C. L. T. *The Story of Letters and Numbers.* London, 1939.

Pritchard, J. B. *Ancient Near Eastern Texts.* Princeton, N.J.: Princeton University Press, 1950.

ANCIENT EGYPT

Cottrell, L. *Life under the Pharaohs.* New York: Holt, Rinehart & Winston, 1960.

——. *The Lost Pharaohs.* New York: The Philosophical Press, 1950.

Davies, N. M. *Picture-Writing in Ancient Egypt.* London: Oxford University Press, 1958.

Emery, W. B. *Archaic Egypt.* London: Pelican Books, 1961.

Gardiner, A. H. *Egypt of the Pharaohs.* Oxford: The Clarendon Press, 1961.

°——. *Egyptian Grammar.* London: Oxford University Press, 1957.

Glanville, S. R. K. *The Legacy of Egypt.* Oxford: The Clarendon Press, 1953.

Kees, H. *Ancient Egypt.* London: Faber and Faber, 1961.

Murray, M. A. *The Splendour That Was Egypt.* London: Sidgewick and Jackson, 1949.

SUMER, BABYLONIA, ASSYRIA

°Budge, E. A. W. *Rise and Progress of Assyriology.* London, 1925.

*Gadd, C. J. *Stones of Assyria*. London, 1936.

Kramer, S. N. *Sumerian Mythology*. Philadelphia, 1944.

Lloyd, Seton. *Early Anatolia*. London: Penguin Books, 1956.

——. *Foundations in the Dust*. London: Penguin Books, 1955.

Rich, C. J. *Narrative of a Journey to the Site of Babylon*. London, 1939.

Smith, S. *History of Assyria*. London: Chatto and Windus, 1928.

Woolley, C. L. *The Sumerians*. London: Oxford University Press, 1928.

CRETE AND THE AEGAEAN

*Bennett, E. L. *The Minoan Linear Script from Pylos*. Cincinnati: University of Cincinnati Press

*——. *The Pylos Tablets*. Princeton, N.J.: Princeton University Press, 1955.

Chadwick, J. *The Decipherment of Linear B*. Cambridge: Cambridge University Press, 1968.

Cottrell, L. *The Bull of Minos*. New York: Holt, Rinehart & Winston, 1958.

*Palmer, L. *Mycenaean Greek Texts*. Oxford: Clarendon Press, 1963.

——. *Mycenaeans and Minoans*. London: Faber and Faber, 1965.

*Ventris, M. *The Knossos Tablets*. London: University of London, Institute of Classical Studies, 1964.

——, and J. Chadwick. *Documents in Mycenaean Greek*. Cambridge: Cambridge University Press, 1956.

Wace, A. J. B. *Mycenae, an Archaeological History and Guide*. Princeton, N.J.: Princeton University Press

INDEX

❧ INDEX

Index

Index

Index